"I have been a financial pl: [vered] thousands of questions. Ur [cated] financial situations is that ([David] have combined their indivi(....a very helpful and practical book. I recommend it highly."

—Ron Blue, founder of Ronald Blue Trust and the Ron Blue Institute of Financial Planning, author of more than twenty books, including *Master Your Money*

"This is a book every blended family needs. It provides practical help in the often difficult area of money management. I highly recommend it."

—Gary D. Chapman, PhD, author of *The 5 Love Languages*

"When developing material on money management and marriage relationships we turned to Ron Deal for expertise on blended family finances. Now you can turn to him. Together with Greg Pettys and David Edwards, Ron has created *The Smart Stepfamily Guide to Financial Planning*. This book integrates practical wisdom of stepfamily relationship dynamics with proven principles of money management and estate planning specifically for stepfamilies."

—Howard Dayton, founder of Compass and *MoneyWise Radio*, cofounder of Crown Financial Ministries

"This exceptionally well-written book is invaluable for many types of 'blended' families. It is comprehensive in that it covers a broad swath of real-life family fiscal matters. The book's authors handily guide us from scenarios where 'everyone has their hands in each other's pockets' to one of structure, clarity, and harmony."

—Greg Dewald, CEO, Bright!Tax, Inc.

"Unspoken money issues lurk in the background of most stepfamily unease and conflict. I wish there were enough research-based trained professionals to help you with these problems, but there are not. For the best and most comprehensive resource available today, use *The Smart Stepfamily Guide to Financial Planning* to identify, discuss, and resolve these difficult topics—a gift beyond measure for your entire family."

—Margorie Engel, MBA (finance), PhD (law and social policy); former president, Stepfamily Association of America; founding member, National Stepfamily Resource Center (NSRC) and Stepfamily Expert Council

"As with all of Ron Deal's work with stepfamilies, this book gives wonderful, wise, practical advice. Every stepfamily needs to know how to successfully navigate the unique challenges they face with finances, and this book is an excellent guide to get you there."

—Shaunti Feldhahn, social researcher and bestselling author of *For Women Only* and *Men, Women, & Money*

"The coauthors do a wonderful job of covering all the important financial decisions one will encounter throughout one's life. This is a must-read for someone searching for a pragmatic financial direction in their life."

—Bernard Shaughnessy, CFP®

"Finances can be a touchy and intimidating subject in any setting, and blended families face unique challenges in this arena. Thankfully, there's a book that will help answer their questions and give them peace of mind—and this is it! Here is a practical, insightful, and relevant resource for stepfamilies."

—Greg Smalley, PsyD, vice president, Marriage and Family Formation, Focus on the Family

THE
SMART
STEPFAMILY
GUIDE TO
FINANCIAL PLANNING

SMART
STEPFAMILY
SERIES

Books in the Smart Stepfamily Series

THE
SMART
STEPFAMILY
GUIDE TO
FINANCIAL PLANNING

Money Management
Before and After You Blend a Family

RON L. DEAL,
GREG S. PETTYS, AND
DAVID O. EDWARDS

BETHANYHOUSE
a division of Baker Publishing Group
Minneapolis, Minnesota

Published by Bethany House Publishers
11400 Hampshire Avenue South
Bloomington, Minnesota 55438
www.bethanyhouse.com

Bethany House Publishers is a division of
Baker Publishing Group, Grand Rapids, Michigan

Printed in the United States of America

Library of Congress Cataloging-in-Publication Data
Names: Deal, Ron L., author. | Pettys, Greg, author. | Edwards, David O., author.
Title: The smart stepfamily guide to financial planning : money management
    before and after you blend a family / Ron L. Deal, Greg S. Pettys, and David O.
    Edwards.
Description: Bloomington, Minnesota : Bethany House Publishers, [2019]
Identifiers: LCCN 2019019791 | ISBN 9780764233357 (trade paper) | ISBN
    9781493421855 (e-book)
Subjects: LCSH: Stepfamilies. | Finance, Personal.
Classification: LCC HQ759.92 .D4165 2019 | DDC 306.874/7—dc23
LC record available at https://lccn.loc.gov/2019019791

All names and recognizable details have been changed to protect the privacy of those who have shared their stories for this book.

This publication is designed to provide general information in regard to the subject matter covered. It is not to be considered tax, legal, or other professional advice. The views and opinions expressed are those of the authors. This publication discusses many strategies and techniques that may not be appropriate for every situation. You should consult with your personal advisors, to include tax and legal, before making any decisions based on the content of this book.

Cover design by Eric Walljasper

Ron L. Deal is represented by MacGregor Literary, Inc.

19 20 21 22 23 24 25   7 6 5 4 3 2 1

Dedication

Ron
To Dr. Margorie Engel, for being the first to open my
eyes to the challenges of stepfamily dynamics and money
matters and for leading the way to practical solutions

Greg
To my wonderful wife, Johnita R. Pettys, God's
amazing covenant gift I will forever treasure

David
To Michelle, Bailey, and Cole, and to
my parents, Delbert and Pat

Contents

Contents

Acknowledgments

Ron:

This book is the result of two influential conversations for which I am very grateful. The first occurred twenty years ago with Dr. Margorie Engel, former president and CEO of the Stepfamily Association of America. Her early writings on money management innovated solutions for stepfamilies, but it was a personal conversation with her that awakened my interest in this subject and started the process that resulted in this book. Just a few years later, I had dinner with Greg Pettys, one coauthor of this book. As a financial planner with a blended family of his own, he was very interested in this subject and shared many ideas that provide the foundation of this book. We both walked away from that conversation saying, "We should write a book someday." We did.

Appreciations to my agent, Chip MacGregor, and editor Beth Jusino (who did the initial painstaking work of helping three voices become one). And thanks to editor Ellen Chalifoux for once again making my books read much better than they were written.

And finally, a special thank-you to Bethany House for investing in stepfamilies around the world by collaborating with me to create the SMART STEPFAMILY SERIES. Your dedication to publishing practical resources to help an underserved people group is admirable. I am honored once again to partner with you.

David:

I remember the day Greg came to my law office asking if I would help him with some content for a breakout session he was doing at one of Ron's stepfamily events. That was the beginning of my journey with Greg and Ron to create a resource to help stepfamilies make wise financial choices.

Thank you to all the blended family clients who have honored me by trusting me to help them plan effectively. My contribution to this book is the result of what I have learned from working with these wonderful families over the years.

Thank you to Ron and Greg. I am honored and humbled to be a part of this project, and I pray that it can be used by many families to make wise decisions that honor God.

Thank you to editor Beth Jusino, who helped immensely in the writing of the healthcare and estate planning chapters.

Greg:

Special thanks to my coauthor friends, Ron L. Deal and David O. Edwards. Ron, your writing expertise, wisdom, and true servant leadership were the glue that kept this project together. David, the combination of your integrity, compassion, and professional excellence amazes me. Both our award-winning developmental editor Beth Jusino and the indispensable Ellen Chalifoux at Bethany House are so appreciated. Sincere gratitude to three mentors who imparted much wisdom to me over these decades of my financial services career: Michael J. Haglin, Bernie Shaughnessy, and Brian Roberts. Heartfelt hugs to each of my six children: Daniel, Kara, James, Kyle, Alicia, and Blake, whose powerful and diverse gifts have inspired me to write! To God be all glory.

Introduction

Imagine a conversation between two people who have been dating for over a year. They are both single parents. After a nice, romantic dinner, he reaches across the table to hold her hand, looks deeply into her eyes, and says, "We've been together a long time, and I can see our futures merging together."

Her heart quickens. Her eyes widen. She nods and leans toward him. *He's going to pop the question!*

"So I," he says and clears his throat, "was wondering . . ."

"Yes?"

"Would you . . ."

"Yes?"

"Outline all of your debts and assets, show me your credit report, and sign this prenuptial agreement?"

Ouch, what a way to spoil an evening—and maybe a relationship. And yet at some point, every couple needs to talk about their values related to money and how they will logistically combine incomes, debt, and the future care of their children. If they don't, blended family money matters might spoil more than an evening.

Among the three of us, we have over fifty years of combined experience with financial planning and blended family education.

We've seen firsthand how money can help bring security to a relationship, and how it can threaten it. What makes the difference is how the couple handles the conversation.

This book is about so much more than money. It's about planning for your future, merging your families, and guarding your marriage. It's about building a loving relationship, based on trust, that provides a safe harbor for you and your children. It's about a harmonious relationship of respect that guides how both of you manage your assets and that turns money into a tool that serves what you value, provides for your family, and prepares your children for healthy adult living.

If that's what you're after, keep reading.

What You May Fear

By the time most people enter a blended family marriage, they and their kids have been beat up by life a little (maybe a lot). Amanda sure was.[1] That's why, when she entered a new relationship, she decided to cohabit with her boyfriend and not marry him. She explained her reasons in a post on social media: "When you divorce, you can lose EVERYTHING. That is so traumatic that you prefer to cohabit [the next time] rather than marry and risk financial (and other) devastation."

Whether you agree with Amanda's life choices or not, many of you can relate to her concerns. You, too, want to protect your children and avoid getting hurt again. And since financial issues can be a landmine topic in relationships, you may also fear

- That money will bring distress. (You know that a high percentage of couples argue about money, and you're *done* with conflict; your previous relationships gave you enough to last a lifetime.)
- That money will divide. (Conflict leads to disaffection and distrust . . . then divorce.)

- That money will destroy. (You're trying to rebuild your life—not experience more pain.)

Can you relate to any of these concerns?

Financing Your Togetherness

Our objective is to help you make money an asset to your relationship, not a liability. Said another way, we want to give you the tools to finance your togetherness, envision your combined financial future, and plan for how you'll get there. We'll also give you practical suggestions for protecting your marriage while doing so. Throughout the book we'll offer first steps for those just getting started and more advanced next steps for those a little further down the financial road. The material here is applicable whether you're widowed or divorced, young or marrying much later in life.

The book is arranged in three parts: "Laying the Groundwork," "Merging Day-to-Day Financial Responsibilities and Relationships," and "Planning for the Future." The first section helps you take stock of your current situation and begin to look down the road, developing a shared vision for how you will get there. In part 2 we'll examine how to merge the day-to-day financial aspects of blended family living while merging relationships as well. And finally, part 3 will help you plan for your financial future, that is, yours and your children's.

Your contribution is to let love lead, especially in money issues. Whether you are dating, engaged, or already married, put on patience and kindness as you learn about and discuss good financial management. Love, like financial investing, always involves risk. The most mature lovers embrace that. They give of themselves even when they aren't sure the other will give back, they are vulnerable even at times of relational uncertainty, and they look for ways to serve the "usness" of their relationship before serving themselves. All of this is risky on some level, both financially and relationally.

However, if your relationship is going to grow, then sacrifice, vulnerability, and a giving heart are unavoidable and necessary risks. Facing the emotional and financial risk *together* is a key way you foster the safe harbor relationship you seek.

How to Use This Book

We highly suggest that couples, whether married or contemplating a joint future, read this book together. Digesting the material at the same time allows you to share your insights and discuss the applications to your family circumstances. If you're a single parent not in a relationship right now and you picked up this book as a way to proactively plan for the future, good for you! The following chapters will provide solid financial advice that will help you develop strategies to care for yourself and your children.

Throughout the book we explore various blended family circumstances. Feel free to skip to the sections that most address yours. For example, young families can apply every chapter, but later-life couples with an empty nest may jump over the chapter about college funding (unless you are saving for your grandchildren); take special note, though, of the sections pertaining to retirement and transferring wealth to your children.

Finally, while this book touches on the relational matters that financial decisions bring up in stepfamilies, primarily it's about the practical issues of money management and estate planning, with an eye toward how those impact your relationships. There are many other resources that primarily address how to strengthen your blended family and your marriage, while giving some consideration to the role money plays. For example, Ron has authored/coauthored a series of books and a DVD series beginning with *The Smart Stepfamily*. This book provides a comprehensive guide to becoming an emotionally and spiritually healthy blended family. *The Smart Stepfamily Marriage*, written with David Olson, is specifically designed to strengthen your marriage, *The Smart*

Stepdad and *The Smart Stepmom* with Laura Petherbridge equip stepparents for success in their roles, and *Dating and the Single Parent* helps couples date well and prepare for marriage while considering the needs of their children. These and other resources and online articles can be found at FamilyLife.com/blended and SmartStepfamilies.com.

PART ONE

Laying the Groundwork

Every good strategic plan begins with an honest assessment of where you are and how you will work together to move forward. In this section we'll help you take stock of your current financial and family situation and give you a system to structure your finances and strengthen your marriage.

1

Taking Stock

. . . and they lived happily ever after.

In the movies, that's often the last line as the couple rides off into the sunset. Unfortunately, we never get to see how they live. The devil, as they say, is in the details. There's no *happily ever after* if you don't know how to live.

Falling in love with a person is easy, but how *all of you* live together—adults, kids, ex-spouses, ex-in-laws, new in-laws, stepsiblings—determines your happily-ever-after. For many blended families, money is a point of convergence for the pain of the past and the uncertainty of the present. But it doesn't have to be that way.

Taking stock of yourself and your family relationships is an important first step to developing a financial vision for your blended family. Since stepfamilies are born out of loss (the death of a parent or the dissolution of the parents' relationship), understanding the past is important in understanding how your blended family will function in the present.

As we shared in the introduction, we want to help you make money an asset to your family, not a liability. We want money

21

management to be something you do *with* and *for* your spouse, not *to* your spouse. And we want estate planning to be something that brings you and your stepchildren together, rather than pushes you apart. So in this chapter, let's take stock of your situation and start to develop a vision for your future together.

Taking Stock of You

So, how are you? No, really, *how are you?*

If we asked God to do an audit of your career, personal relationships, habits, behaviors, marriage, family, and emotional well-being, how would it turn out?

We're not asking if you are perfect (we already know the answer to that one). Instead, we're inviting you to pause and assess your overall health and well-being. Are you rooted in the eternal, or are you living for today? Are you free to enjoy life, or are you imprisoned by an addiction? Are your relationships safe and life-giving, or are you paralyzed by insecurity?

Why does this matter? Because everything is connected. Eventually, you and your partner are going to discuss family and finances, and if they can't trust you because of a bad attitude or habit you can't shake, then making decisions about your financial future is going to be difficult.

We're not trying to make you feel bad about yourself. However, it's very important that you be honest with yourself. Take a minute, pause, and reflect on the question "How are you?" If you want, use the space below to write your reflections as you take stock.

_____

_____

_____

_____

_____

Taking Stock of Your Blended Family

A stepfamily, also called a blended family, is a complex spaghetti of loyalties, cultures, traditions, DNA, expectations, parenting styles, losses, fears, and people—both those in the home and outside the home (like ex-spouses and adult children). Merging as a stepfamily means merging all of these pieces. Family harmony and peace come when the parts and pieces bond and integrate.

A wedding that forms a stepfamily clearly defines the couple's relationship as "committed till death do us part," but it's less clear how children (adult or young), former spouses, grandparents, in-laws, and all the rest will be a family. The desire of a couple to blend does not magically produce a family smoothie—it takes work, cooperation, and collaboration to bond stepparents and stepchildren and integrate family narratives. And that's if everyone is equally open and willing to try. You can imagine, or perhaps you already know firsthand, what it's like if some are and some aren't.

What does this have to do with financial planning and money management? Everything. Before marriage if one parent offered their children an allowance as a reward for completing chores, but the other parent did not, which system will they use in their stepfamily? Assuming at least one parent (and maybe both) has to make changes, will their children resent the changes? Will they refuse to accept the transition?

You see, underneath many financial conflicts in stepfamilies are much bigger issues of belonging, loyalty, trust, power, control, acceptance, perceptions of favoritism, and fears of relational uncertainty.

Sandra, a divorced mother of two, faced a dilemma like this. Dave, her second husband of five years, wanted her to change her will and leave everything to him. Dave didn't have children of his own, so naming Sandra as his sole beneficiary was a simple decision. But Sandra was concerned about her sons. They were already in their early twenties and living independently when Dave came into her life, so while Dave and her sons got along well enough, they never really bonded. Sandra wasn't confident that Dave would take care of them financially if she died, or that they would even let him.

On the surface, this seems to be a question about Sandra's will. But underlying that question are a lack of family integration, loyalty conflicts (Does Sandra choose her husband or sons?), and issues of marital trust. Factors like these influence a blended family's financial decisions far more than math or principles of investing.

Said another way, financial conflicts are often just a symptom of much deeper blended family dynamics and relationships.

A thorough exploration of stepfamily development and dynamics is beyond the scope of this book.[1] But take a minute to reflect on the following questions to help you get a clear picture of your current family situation.

- Are you rushing or did you rush to the altar? A short dating season and a hurried wedding do not give anyone much time to prepare for or adjust to a healthy stepfamily. You may have to deal with deeply held resentments from the children toward their parent or stepparent or suspicion from other family members. Slow down. Let time be your friend, and give lots of consideration to the needs of your children.

- Do you have unreasonably high expectations about family bonding and harmony? Integrating a blended family into a cohesive unit takes most stepfamilies years. Expecting love or trust to happen too fast sets everyone up for disappointment. Be intentional to build connection, but also be patient with the bonding process.

- How strong is your couple relationship or marriage? Stepfamily stress caused by new relationships, ex-spouses, conflicts with children, parenting disagreements, and more will ripple into a couple's relationship. It's not easy to simultaneously carry stress and lead your family through it—all while developing harmony in your marriage. But a stepfamily without a strong marital relationship is doomed.

- Are you working as a capable parenting team? When there are co-parents (biological parents living in separate homes), many stepfamilies find themselves with multiple adults trying to parent multiple children in multiple homes. Things can get difficult quickly. Your first priority should be that the parent-stepparent team in your home works well together. You simply can't work through the integration process without unity. If the other parent is still in your child's life, it's also important to work toward basic respect and cooperation between homes.

- Are there other common pitfalls that are creating issues for you at this point? Perhaps you struggle with unacknowledged feelings of loss, unexpressed grief, difficulty merging traditions, or being controlled by guilt or fear. These can all spill over into the way you view and handle money matters.

- Are you fighting a temptation to give up? It's a shame, but most redivorces occur when one or both partners quit too quickly. The average stepfamily, as we said, needs many years to solidify their relationships and experience rewards, but a high percentage of remarried couples divorce within two years. They quit before things get good. Don't fall into that pit; be determined. Keep going.

With these questions in front of you, take a minute to pause and reflect. Use the space below to take stock of your blended family and discuss what you can do to learn more about healthy stepfamily living.[2]

Taking Stock of Your Values about Money

Before we start talking about specific numbers, we also need to take stock of your values, specifically about financial matters, and how they converge with your spouse's.

You might have heard that many divorces are caused by conflicts about money. Actually, money is just the surface issue. In addition to relational dynamics, it's things like differences in our *underlying values* that cause conflict, not money. For example, in their book *Your New Money Mindset*, authors Brad Hewitt and James Moline point out that the value of consumerism—the "obsession with money and all that it can buy"—impacts how people manage their money and their relationship to money.[3] Hewitt and Moline describe a study of the super-rich, which found that even the majority of people with at least $25 million in assets didn't think they had enough money; they reported needing at least 25 percent more in order to be secure.[4] By contrast, the authors point out that those with a healthy relationship with money felt more peaceful about their situation, no matter how much they had, and likely were more generous.

As you can imagine, if one partner values consumerism and the other values generosity, the couple will have difficulty finding common ground in financial planning and making daily money decisions.

Objectively taking stock of our values is more difficult than it seems. You may find it helpful to take a free online assessment at NewMoneyMindset.com called "Your New Money Mindset" from Brad Hewitt and James Moline. This will give you greater insight into your money attitudes and values.

Once you've completed that, talk through the following questions about your values with your partner. Though not an exhaustive list, these questions will help you identify any gaps in your values. These are the areas where you will inevitably experience conflict, so you might as well be proactive to talk through them.

- Are you generally satisfied with what you have, and do you live within your means?
- Is generosity (sharing money, time, or energy with others) a priority for you?
- How do religious beliefs impact your decisions about and attitude toward money? For example, are you a steward of your money, or the owner? Give examples of how this has played out in your life.
- When it comes to material things that depreciate (clothes, cars, computers, etc.) do you value buying new or used? Does it need to be the latest and greatest model?
- What makes sacrificing something material that you want worth it and why?
- For you, does the amount of money you have represent status, security, enjoyment, control, or provision so you can fulfill your purpose? Why?
- Do you believe that people should work to earn their money? Is it important to "learn the value of a dollar"? What might this look like in parenting?
- Which do you find yourself pursuing or longing for when it comes to money: contentment with what you have or having more?
- What would you say to those who suggest that debt is a form of servitude? When is it okay to take on debt?
- What is your attitude about giving to individuals, your church, and other nonprofits and charities? What has been your practice?

- What have you taught your children about money?
- When is it okay to give or loan money to family members? Should there be conditions?
- Are you a spender or a saver, and why? (Now answer the question from the point of view of others: Would your parents say you are a spender or a saver? What would your friends or previous spouse say? What would your children say?)
- What are you saving for? Is retirement something you're planning for, and what do you think it looks like?
- How much independence should there be in a marriage when it comes to financial decisions? For example, how much can you spend without consulting/informing the other?
- Currently, what do you consider "my money," "your money," and "our money"?

Talking through these questions will likely uncover stories from your past, including moments of joy and pain in your life, and give perspective to your current financial situation and how you got here. Do not rush through this discussion.

In fact, you may need multiple conversations with your partner to spend adequate time on each question. Again, the point is to take stock of the values behind each of your individual histories and decide if you will keep them going forward. You will return to these values repeatedly while applying the principles of this book. Write your observations here.

_____

_____

_____

_____

_____

Taking Stock of Your Financial Situation

You can't set out for a destination without first knowing where you're starting from. Many couples, even some who have been married for some time, have never sat down to look at and understand their current financial situation.

In the next chapter you'll examine your current situation in detail, but for now, start thinking about a few significant aspects. What are your major assets and remaining debts? Who are the people you are financially responsible for (e.g., children) or to (e.g., aging parents)? What happens to all this if one of you dies?

Again, you'll outline this in detail later, but for now, what jumps out to you as something you need to organize or decide together?[5]

Getting Started

Now that you've taken time to reflect on your story, you can carry these insights with you as you move through the book. In the next chapter, we'll show you a key ingredient to getting smart with your finances—a plan, if you will, that will provide the scaffolding to help you finance togetherness.

But a quick word of caution before we do: Since every blended family story is different, every financial situation and solution will also be different. As you read the stories of others and learn from their circumstances, keep in mind that your story is unique and will need unique solutions. If the conversations you've had thus far are more challenging than you anticipated, or if the strategies in the following chapters seem overwhelming, consider seeking out a personal financial planner or estate attorney to guide you through the process of creating your unique financial plan.

2

Creating a Togetherness
Agreement

n 2016 a home designer in the Netherlands introduced a new concept for a floating prenuptial house. Its purpose, in our opinion, is rather ominous. According to a *Dezeen* article by Jessica Mairs, the units, designed like two Tetris shapes, "break apart, so unhappily married occupants can cast their spouses adrift."[1] We call that planning to fail.

What if you turned that idea upside down and took the two separate, Tetris-like shapes of your financial house and secured them firmly together? Instead of planning to fail, you could carefully orchestrate your financial circumstances into an interlocked design that would merge your lives and financial future. We call that planning to succeed.

In this chapter, we'll introduce you to the Togetherness Agreement, or TA, a strategy that brings clarity to some of the most emotionally charged issues for couples while reaffirming their commitment to the permanency of their marriages.[2]

Togetherness Agreements, which can be created before or after you marry, are not for every couple, but if created in the right spirit, they provide a framework for a detailed vision of an optimistic future together.

Financing Togetherness

Marcus and Alisa were ready to take the plunge. Both had been married before and both had kids, and now they were excited to plan a life together. Still, marriage was a scary proposition. Kids, schedules, ways of doing things, money, future plans . . . there were lots of things they knew they needed to discuss and plan for, and also plenty of issues they'd have to figure out as they went along.

The week after he and Alisa got engaged, Marcus went to breakfast with his friend Steve, who had been through his own divorce and remarriage a few years before. "You need to make sure you do a prenuptial agreement before the wedding to cover your legal bases," Steve advised. Marcus hadn't considered this before, but Steve's advice sounded like a normal thing that any wise person would do.

So later that week, when Marcus met Alisa for lunch, he raised the issue. Alisa was a manager in retail and smart about financial issues, so Marcus reasoned that she would quickly agree that this was a good idea. As their waiter brought their food, Marcus casually said, "Steve suggested we make a prenuptial agreement, just to take care of details and plan ahead."

"What?" Alisa's expression was shocked, and then angry. "If you aren't committed to this relationship and to combining our families, then maybe we need to rethink the whole thing!" With that, she stormed off to the bathroom.

When Alisa returned, things were very tense. Marcus didn't mention the prenup again. They got through lunch, and each went on with their day. Later, Alisa met her friend Maria to talk about planning the church's women's retreat.

"Is anything wrong?" Maria asked. "It seems like something's bothering you."

Alisa told her friend, who had also been divorced, about Marcus's prenup comment.

Maria's eyes flared. "Why would he say that? Just so he can divorce you and leave you high and dry?"

Alisa and Maria aren't alone. For a lot of people, the word *prenup* is nothing but negative. Basically, we agree. But perhaps there is something within the idea that is worth salvaging.

Making a detailed plan for your future is a good idea; you just need to do so in a way that facilitates togetherness. A prenuptial agreement is a contract entered into prior to marriage that commonly includes direction on the division of property and various types of support in the event of divorce. Most law students are required to take a contract law class during their first year of law school. Why? Because contracts are everywhere. Some are in writing; some are not. Some are fulfilled right away; others aren't completed until a time far into the future. Every time you buy or sell anything, you make a contract, whether you know it or not. This might include buying gas at the gas station, signing up for a health club membership, or agreeing to buy a house.

In other words, not all contracts are bad. What if Marcus and Alisa could make a contract or agreement that financed togetherness, instead of isolation? What if you could plan for your marriage and your children's financial futures and foster confidence in your relationship and emotional security, instead of guardedness and insecurity?

To do that, we suggest you create a Togetherness Agreement, a detailed financial vison of your life together. Essentially, it involves putting everything on the financial table—your assets, debts, dreams, and obligations—and deciding how you can meet your needs and facilitate the permanency of your marriage. This takes work, but the net result is a stronger relationship. Like an employee contract is meant to provide for the employee while he or she works with the company, the Togetherness Agreement provides for your positive and secure future together.

Some will choose to have their Togetherness Agreement (TA) drafted by a lawyer so that it is binding (a legal contract). It's best to find someone who is experienced with blended families and shares a positive focus for the Togetherness Agreement. Others will be satisfied to talk through the matter on their own (with or without an attorney) and design a path forward. Both create a shared vision for life together.

We think making the TA legally binding is ideal for many reasons. For example, it sets in stone for future generations your intentions should something tragic happen to you. Children and stepchildren don't always share the same values as their parents when it comes to inheritance. Also, we find that couples are more intentional to live by their own agreement when there is a third party (in this case, the state) holding them accountable.

The specific stipulations included in a Togetherness Agreement vary by couple but will give consideration to your blended family. Your TA might include general agreements about handling finances as well as agreements regarding the financial support, rights, roles, responsibilities, and overall well-being of spouses, children, stepchildren, grandchildren, stepgrandchildren, parents, stepparents, grandparents, stepgrandparents, and other significant relationships. It's not just about money; it's a plan for how money will help care for your family over time.

Once drafted, a Togetherness Agreement serves as a valuable document for your financial planner, if you have one. They'll be able to keep a keen eye on your entire life plan and over time help everyone involved efficiently implement your well-designed plan. This will help give you confidence that all of your blended family goals will be carried out.

The Togetherness Agreement in Action

Perhaps the best way to explain the value of a Togetherness Agreement is to see one in action.

Anthony and Jenny are planning for their marriage. Anthony has two young boys from a previous marriage, and Jenny has a teenage daughter. They both would like to have at least two more children together.

Anthony, forty-four, is a successful construction company owner. He also recently received a modest inheritance from his deceased aunt. He has had difficulty keeping debt out of his life.

Jenny is a thirty-six-year-old CPA (certified public accountant) who is very good at budgeting money but has few assets. She cares for her elderly mother, who is generally healthy but recently started to forget some important things. Jenny is concerned that she may soon need to make good on her promise to move her mom in with her.

Anthony's ex-wife has made it clear that she will not allow him to take the boys out of the state and, furthermore, that they will have to attend in-state colleges. Jenny never hears from or sees her ex-husband, who has had legal problems. Because of him, there is a lien on their still jointly owned home.

Anthony dreads telling Jenny that when he passes away, he wants his construction company and any assets, including the inheritance, to go to his children instead of Jenny. He is willing to make provision for her and her daughter, but he wants his biological children to maintain control of his business and inheritance.

When they sit down to work out their Togetherness Agreement, many of these issues come up. Jenny finds out about Anthony's damaged credit rating because of his past debt, and he discovers that his future mother-in-law may come live with them. Anthony also communicates his desires for the future of his business.

What does the creation of a Togetherness Agreement do for this couple? Primarily, it allows Anthony and Jenny a time of full and complete discovery and a framework to discuss all of their financial matters with integrity and transparency. Because they are both open about their situations, they can agree that these challenges are just speed bumps that can be overcome and move into their marriage with open eyes.

Working on a TA is also the opportunity Anthony and Jenny need to discuss solutions like purchasing long-term care insurance for Jenny's mother in order to work toward assisted living support if she needs it. Together with their attorney, they work out a qualified terminable interest property trust, or QTIP*, that spells out provisions for Jenny's and Anthony's children in the event of his death.

Finally, the Togetherness Agreement helps them address how they plan to manage money on a daily basis: Jenny will take oversight of their joint budget, and they will share a joint savings account. They agree that each will maintain 40 percent of their liquid assets in separate accounts for five years while other issues related to Anthony's debt are worked out. They also agree that Anthony will seek counseling and become accountable for rebuilding his credit.

In the end, the TA provides this couple peace of mind in terms of finances and their relationship, and it does so based on love, respect, and compassionate commitments.

Is a TA Right for You?

In our combined professional experience, a Togetherness Agreement is especially valuable for couples in blended families, where issues are often complex. It's a chance to take your marital vows to another level and bring much-needed detail. One couple described it as "writing the rules for our marriage."

Ideally, a Togetherness Agreement is something you work out before you enter marriage. But there's no rule that says that's the only

---

* A qualified terminable interest property trust (QTIP) is an increasingly popular choice for parents in blended families who need to juggle various priorities and family needs, because it allows a person to assign assets to a surviving spouse for the duration of their lifetime, exempt from estate taxes, and then specify that the assets in the QTIP get passed on to the beneficiary of your choice—your children, grandchildren, church, charity, etc.—upon the spouse's death. In other words, it has the unique quality of allowing you to control your assets from the grave, caring for both your spouse and children. For more information about trusts, see chapter 11 and appendix 3, "QTIP Trust Case Study."

time for it. It's never too late to sit down and talk openly and honestly about your financial strengths, weaknesses, and questions.

If you're like most couples, you have a lot of life experience already under your belts. You've built wealth, or perhaps you've built debt. You may have complicated or hard-to-value assets. And there are children's needs and futures to consider. What is each partner's financial commitment to the children in your relationship?

In addition, couples facing specific situations can address them through a Togetherness Agreement. For example:

- If you or your partner owns or foresees someday owning a business or professional practice, having a Togetherness. Agreement is a way to address, as a couple, how the business will be handled in the event of the business owner's death or incapacitation.

- If you expect to one day receive a sizable inheritance, having a Togetherness Agreement could alleviate any questions or concerns about how that will be distributed, both for you and for the person who will eventually delegate the inheritance.

- If you're currently parenting young children, a TA could spell out your desire for one parent to stay home full-time and also address how a single income will be managed, both right away and in the event that one spouse dies.

- If you're entering into a marriage later in life, the TA helps you grapple with questions about retirement or long-term care.

Togetherness Agreements can also be especially helpful with these five types of marital properties discussed by lawyer Nihara Choudhri in her book *What to Do before "I Do"*:

1. Pensions and other retirement benefits
2. Stock options

3. Professional licenses and degrees
4. Closely held corporations and other businesses
5. Professional goodwill[3]

Let's look at each of these in more detail.

Pensions and Other Retirement Benefits

Pensions and other retirement benefits are usually where the largest concentration of blended family net worth exists. This includes defined benefit pension plans as well as defined contribution plans such as IRAs, SEPs, 401(k)s, 403(b)s, and other qualified retirement plans. Since most states view pensions and retirement plans as joint marital property, and there are many complex ERISA[4] rules that govern them, going beyond simple beneficiary designations to include some guidance in a Togetherness Agreement can be a very positive step in financial planning for the blended family.

James and Keesha had no intention of splitting up, but when they sat down to work out their TA they both agreed that the future of the pension was something to address, because each had already been burned by long-term, messy financial disputes and entanglements in their first marriages. (To see how James and Keesha maximized James's pension in concert with a life insurance policy, see appendix 1, "Pension Options Case Study.")

Their financial advisor helped them explore different methods of dividing pension and retirement plans cleanly and simply. One would be for James to buy out Keesha's pension share with a lump sum cash payment or other marital assets if the marriage dissolved, based on how long they were together. The second option, which James and Keesha agreed made the most sense, was for James to agree in the TA that he would pay Keesha only if and when the pension vested, using a qualified domestic relations order, or QDRO. While neither of them expected to need this clause of their agreement, discussing what was fair and equitable was a good process for them to help build their communication skills and align their values.

There are myriad other retirement options for blended family couples to consider when designing a TA, based on individual situations. We'll talk about a few in chapter 9.

Professional Licenses and Degrees

Both divorced, Ryan and Debra married during Debra's first year of medical school. Ryan has a young daughter from his previous marriage, and he and Debra now have two more children of their own. He loves his teaching job, and it put bread on the table during Debra's eight years of medical school and residency.

When Ryan and Debra discussed their financial goals and plans for their blended family, she wanted to make up to him in a tangible way all he had done to support her in those early days. They met with their attorney to create what is known as a spousal lifetime access trust, or SLAT. It is an irrevocable trust designed to get money out of the donor's estate for estate tax purposes, but at the same time allowing the beneficiary spouse access to the trust funds during his or her lifetime for health, education, support, and maintenance. Then at that beneficiary spouse's passing, the remaining trust proceeds flow to their named beneficiaries. Debra gifted some money into this SLAT and then outlined in the Togetherness Agreement her purpose for supporting Ryan and ultimately leaving trust proceeds equally to all of their children and grandchildren.

Stock Options

An employee stock option is a right given by a company to an employee to buy company stock at a fixed or discounted price. If you are fortunate enough to have these financial instruments in your portfolio, having a clearly outlined Togetherness Agreement could be advantageous. This is because courts usually consider all forms of alternative compensation, such as corporate stock options, as marital property. However, it's definitely not that simple. In fact, stock options can be very complex, taking more than one form and having many variables. For example, Marshall was given some of his stock options before his marriage to his second wife, Marianne, as incentives for him to work hard. Other options given after Marshall and Marianne were married were rewards for Marshall's past hard work. The question of what part of these financial instruments was earned during their marriage leaves much room for confusion and contention. What if he intends for those options earned prior to their marriage to go to his son from his first marriage but has never discussed this with Marianne? Perhaps he wants that son to have everything earned prior to their marriage and wants the rest to go to charity. The problem is that Marianne has no idea about either of these possible intentions.

One of the items that Marshall and Marianne wrote up in their Togetherness Agreement was a stock option directives section. In these paragraphs, Marshall clearly outlined all of the options in his portfolio and where he wanted proceeds from each option series to eventually go, whether to the son from his previous marriage or his favorite charity. In lieu of the options, Marianne would receive proceeds from a paid-up life insurance policy she would own on Marshall.[5] This gave Marshall the privilege of making his intentions clear and gave Marianne peace of mind by removing all uncertainty about this issue.

Closely Held Corporations and Other Businesses

With family-owned businesses there is a great need for clarity about the business's transition upon the death, disability, or divorce of the owner(s). Remember Anthony and Jenny, whom we introduced earlier in the chapter? Anthony was nervous about telling Jenny that he wanted to be sure his construction business, which he started before the couple met, would be passed entirely to his children. Jenny, meanwhile, was busy with her own CPA practice and had no interest in or experience with the construction industry. If Anthony predeceased Jenny without making any plans, she would suddenly be running the company, whether she and Anthony wanted that or not.

Because they were committed to having tough conversations, and by being totally transparent, Anthony and Jenny were able to work out the business transition issues in their Togetherness Agreement. They used a QTIP trust to give Jenny income from some of Anthony's assets at his passing. Upon her death, these assets would eventually go to his children.

For couples like Anthony and Jenny, there is a great need to work through the many variables of business transition. These include having a written buy-sell agreement, having the proper types and amounts of insurance to protect key people and property, and coordinating all survivor responsibilities in the event of death, disability, or other contingencies. Without such planning, the surviving spouse often ends up owning and trying to run a company that he or she is not willing or able to run. Proper planning may include a Togetherness Agreement that can tie together all of the many strategies with an overarching, long-range view.

Professional Goodwill

Professional goodwill in a business valuation is the intangible value that is derived from the business's strong reputation, prominent brand awareness, and loyal customer base. This goodwill value is a somewhat complicated component of the worth of a business and therefore is sometimes hard to determine. What is the significance in a blended family of having a properly estimated goodwill value?

Although you may think that your business is worth a certain amount, if the valuation were to be scrutinized at the passing of your spouse, the IRS may think much more highly of the business than you do. This could subject you to additional income tax if the business is sold during your lifetime or federal estate taxes at your spouse's passing.

In addition to a proper business valuation that includes this concept of goodwill, having a Togetherness Agreement could be crucial. The Togetherness Agreement would address the details of the business valuation and all the contingencies of the business transition.

Calvin and Marcella are a blended family couple who purchased an automotive parts business on an acre of land fifteen years ago. Since then they have gathered a growing customer base and their company has become a household name with three locations in key areas. Their initial property is now surrounded by high-end subdivisions. Their buy-sell agreement, written ten years ago, states that Calvin's sons will have first rights of refusal to buy the business with the proceeds from a life insurance policy on their father.

However, as happens with many family business owners, Calvin and Marcella used an inadequate formula that gave their business a valuation without factoring in professional goodwill. Today, with rising property values and the power of their business's name, the IRS would peg the valuation at five times the amount of life insurance provided in the business transition plan. In the event that Calvin predeceases Marcella, his sons will not have the funds to buy their father's business, and Marcella, who has made it clear that she does not want to run the automotive parts business, will be stuck with the company. It will most likely have to be sold for much less than its true value, and the sons will not receive all that their father worked so hard to build up. A Togetherness Agreement could alleviate these problems.

Getting Started

If you are focusing on this chapter prior to tying the knot, congratulations! The TA is especially valuable for a couple just starting their relationship, because it will help you work through questions about the future and uncover things you need to know about one another. However, many couples didn't have time to address these elements of financial planning prior to merging their family. You're just now starting to understand all of the ways that each of your financial histories and situations intersect with your day-to-day lives and decisions. If you've been married for some time, a TA could still help you recommit to your relationship and to transparency. Or you may discover that other tools we discuss later in the book, like trusts (chapters 10 and 11), will better address your needs.

Entering the TA process, whatever the stage of your relationship, requires mutual respect and awareness.

As we saw with the earlier example of Alisa and Marcus, the idea of any written agreement can be a cause for alarm or suspicion for some people, especially if they've been hurt in the past. Is a written agreement a sign of mistrust in your partner? Could even raising the subject potentially damage your relationship?

A Togetherness Agreement must be shared, so it's important not to try to force your partner to enter the process. Doing so could bring harm to the relationship and hurt the trust that you've built.

If you think a Togetherness Agreement would help your marriage, discuss the option with your partner in terms of the net result you are striving for—trust and greater security for both of you. Agree that your goal in this contract is not to plan for divorce, but to address and clarify in advance what might become emotionally charged issues for your blended family down the road, reaffirming your commitment to the permanency of your marriage and providing for your children.

Once you are both on board, seek out an experienced lawyer who can help you draft the document that best reflects your desires.[6] This might cost a few hundred or even a few thousand dollars, depending on your situation and where you live. However, a solid Togetherness Agreement can save multiple times its cost in later legal fees. If cost is a concern, try to discuss the following questions first, as a couple, and come to some foundational agreements before stepping into the attorney's office. The remaining chapters of this book will offer guidance.

- Create an "Own and Owe" list. See appendix 2.
- What is each partner's specific commitment of financial support and physical responsibility for children, stepchildren, grandchildren, stepgrandchildren, parents, stepparents, grandparents, stepgrandparents, and other significant relationships?
- What are the assets of each partner, including property? Are there assets, like a home or college savings account, that are tied to your children, ex-spouse, or another family member? Do you foresee any significant assets being added (through inheritance)?
- What are your current financial debts? What has been your process for paying those off?
- How do you view your current careers, and how will you, as a couple, engage with each other's professional lives? Do you foresee one or both of you making a career sacrifice (staying home to raise children, supporting the family while the other partner pursues an education or launches a business, etc.)? If so, how does that affect your joint future?
- Do you expect to support elderly parents or other family members in need of long-term care? How will that be handled?
- How will day-to-day financial issues be handled in your blended household? Are there specific guidelines or roles you can agree to in budgeting, asset management, and debt management? Should your accounts be joint or separate? How much money is considered "yours"? How much is "ours"?
- Do you each have current estate planning documents? Have you each reviewed the other person's estate plan, and do you understand the roles of and know all of the key members of your financial advisory team?
- If one or both partners own businesses, how do you see the day-to-day management and growth handled? What is the business owner's plan or desire for the future?

44

For Your Spouse, Not *To* Your Spouse

If the idea of a Togetherness Agreement brings up only a negative reaction in your partner or in you, there are two responses you might consider.

First, ask your financial planner if there are other ways to address some of your biggest financial questions and goals. Clarifying your desires in a trust or other estate document may help, as will agreeing in a less formal way how day-to-day expenses and savings will be handled.

Second, recognize that a negative reaction may be an indicator of a deeper fear in your partner or in you. Recognize the fear and articulate it. Put aside conversations about the details of your money matters, and as a couple talk about your past experiences and what's driving strong emotional reactions now. Then you can return to making financial plans.

Remember: A prenuptial agreement is done *to* your spouse when you want to protect yourself in the event of a divorce. A Togetherness Agreement is done *for* your spouse. Better yet, when it is created *with* your spouse, both persons make promises on behalf of the other and lay a positive foundation for their life together.

Relationships and Money

Now that you have a vision for how a Togetherness Agreement can serve your family, let's examine how stepfamily relationships and money impact each other. Ultimately, long-range financial success requires investments in both your family relationships and your portfolio.

Merging Day-to-Day Financial Responsibilities and Relationships

Merging the day-to-day financial aspects of a blended family also includes merging relationships.

The ideal of marriage, we all know, is that two become one. That sounds good until you have two sets of every-thing, from mortgages to children. There are many emotional and practical issues related to merging two families that Ron addresses in his SMART STEPFAMILY SERIES of books (*The Smart Stepfamily, The Smart Stepmom*, etc.). In this section, we'll address some salient relationship dynamics and discuss how they impact money matters.

3

Merging Yours, Mine, and Ours

Merging finances is tied to how you merge relationships in your stepfamily. That might seem obvious, but many people don't connect the dots in everyday life.

Every time Lucinda offered an opinion to her husband, Matt, on the care or discipline of his children, he cut her off and criticized her—often in front of the kids. He sidelined her as an authority figure in their family, insisting on keeping all of the power and control for himself, but at the same time he expected her to provide for the family financially while he put off getting a better-paying job. The former behavior conveyed a message of "my children and I are independent of you," while the latter communicated, "I'm dependent on you."

Matt couldn't have it both ways. Marginalizing his wife relationally while still expecting financial oneness resulted in ever-widening emotional gaps both in their marriage and between Lucinda and her stepchildren. Eventually, Lucinda moved out. When their separation turned into divorce proceedings, Matt demanded that his wife make the process go quickly. She told him if he wanted that, he would have to pay the added attorney fees. She was done supporting him. Ouch.

What's the moral of this story? The emotional music that surrounds the way you deal with money also surrounds your outlook on life, the emotional bonding process of your home, and the quality of connection and communication between you as a couple and your family members.

Do you remember we said in chapter 1 that underneath many financial conflicts in stepfamilies are bigger issues of belonging, loyalty, trust, power, control, acceptance, perceptions of favoritism, and fears of relational uncertainty? Merging finances is always tied to how you merge the relationships in your stepfamily. You must pay attention to the relational dance of your home as much as you count dollars and cents.

Three Pots of Money

In *The Smart Stepfamily*, former president of the Stepfamily Association of America Dr. Margorie Engel explained that there are multiple ways blended family couples pool their daily cash flow. She referred to them as "pots" of money.

The one-pot approach is when couples combine all of their assets, cash flow, and bill paying into accounts owned jointly by both spouses. Two-pot couples take a his-and-hers approach, keeping all of their finances separate, while three-pot couples add joint accounts, which they both contribute to and use to pay specific expenses and save for specific purposes. Joint accounts are used for shared household expenses, investments, car insurance, and vacations, while individual accounts cover personal spending. Each couple decides, based on their situation, whether expenses for children, debt from before the marriage, or other expenses are shared or individual. For one couple we know, the three-pot system was especially helpful because the wife did not like the idea of her husband paying his child support out of her money or even their money. Since the husband had a separate account, he paid his child support from that, and his wife was reassured that she was not involved.

The reactions from readers of *The Smart Stepfamily* to the different models of money management varied widely, even though the book explained that all of the pot systems have merits and have proven successful for many couples.

- "Anyone who's been divorced would be crazy to combine all their money in with their partner's. What if they leave?"
- "We've been living autonomously for years, and our businesses and assets are complex. Why would we go to the hassle of merging them?"
- "Just putting the money together doesn't mean we're together."
- "I thought the point of marriage was oneness. How can couples become one if they keep their money separate?"

This last point was an issue for Jamar and Michelle. She brought two children to their marriage, and he had one son who lived primarily with his mother. Despite meeting through an online dating site that guaranteed them compatibility, they argued frequently during their first year of marriage, especially about money. Michelle wanted to maintain two individual pots of money. Jamar said her lack of commitment to a one-pot system was a commentary on her commitment to the marriage.

"We're not one yet," he told her. "Marriage is about becoming one. The two don't stay two."

Michelle wasn't opposed to the notion of emotional and physical oneness; she just didn't feel a sense of urgency to unite their finances. She drew similar lines when it came to parenting decisions about her children. She wanted to be the final authority on anything related to her kids, explaining that it was important for them to have consistency.

51

Her attitude made Jamar feel separated from her. He believed he wasn't trusted and wasn't as important to her as he wanted to be.

Michelle wasn't trying to shut Jamar out, and as they grew together and he learned more about Michelle's past, he understood more about her apprehensions. Her first husband had abandoned her for another woman and left Michelle with little except debt from a stack of maxed-out credit cards. He'd almost entirely disappeared from his kids' lives. It took her many years to get out from under the constant worry about how she would pay the bills. Now, she admitted, she was guarded and cautious with her finances and children. As a competent professional on a pathway to financial peace, she was hesitant—despite her love for Jamar—to give up control of her bank account again.

The logistics of putting money into one account were just the tip of the iceberg. Merging hearts, futures, and care of their children was a far more emotionally risky endeavor. And how Michelle and Jamar resolved those questions would govern if, when, and how they merged their pots of money.

We've met many couples in blended families who have similar concerns, so let's unpack this further. As we do, ask yourself what fears and concerns you have that underlie your financial decisions to this point. How does fear hold you back from a full merger?

As a child Jamar often felt insignificant to his parents. Then his first wife left him for another man. So when he married Michelle, in the back of his mind he constantly wondered whether she really loved him as much as she said and whether he was emotionally safe with her. This fear set him up for what is called *confirmation bias*, which is seeing what you already believe to be true and ignoring information that refutes your beliefs. This happens, by the way, in every aspect of life, including ways that we manage money. Suppose a friend tells you that they suspect a company you invested in is about to flounder. Despite news and reports that suggest otherwise, you sell your stock. Trust in your friend has biased your viewpoint.

Similarly, Jamar was afraid of trusting Michelle's love for him, and so he interpreted her desire to keep separate accounts as having ulterior motives for holding back from him. Confirmation bias, in effect, led him to apply malignant meanings to the benign actions of his wife. Her hesitation to immediately merge their money was, perhaps, disappointing, but he took it as evidence that she wasn't trustworthy. He saw what he was afraid to see.

Michelle, on the other hand, had good reason to be slow to merge their finances; she had been deeply wounded by her first husband. Left financially high and dry, she vowed that she and her kids would never be put in that position again. Imagine being robbed at knifepoint and having your life threatened. You might become vigilant to never be vulnerable like that again. Michelle was vigilant.

Ultimately, Jamar and Michelle had to determine how many pots of money they would have, but the number of pots they kept didn't necessarily determine the level of security they each felt in the marriage. Couples can have many pots of money or just one combined pot and still trust that the other has their best interest at heart.

To find this trust, Jamar and Michelle had to dip below the surface money matters to deal with their fears and risk-averse behavior.

Above and Below the Surface

Do you have below-the-surface concerns about the long-term stability and security of your marriage or blended family?

A lack of trust will sabotage every above-the-surface strategy a blended family adopts for their day-to-day financial decisions. If you found yourself getting anxious as you considered how to apply the first part of this book, you, too, may have below-the-surface issues to address. That anxiety is telling you something.

When below-the-surface issues come up, it's important for both partners in a relationship to exercise great patience with each other's fears. As Jamar and Michelle came to understand each other's pasts, they found compassion and grace for each other. They lowered their demands related to money and became much more patient with the merging process. Accommodating each other while they continued to work through their fears was an act of love that, ultimately, helped make true oneness more possible.

Unfortunately, most people inadvertently keep themselves stuck in fear. For a long time, Jamar was stuck in his fear that Michelle's hesitation to combine their bank accounts was an indication of her lack of dedication to him. In looking for relational reassurance of her love, he became almost obsessive about her behavior while remaining blind to his own fear. And Jamar is not alone. We've met many people who wait and watch their spouse, hoping that they will see enough evidence of devotion to make their fear go away and the marriage stronger. Of course, "enough" evidence never comes, in part because all spouses make mistakes, but also because confirmation bias prevents the fearful partner from recognizing positive evidence. They only see tainted evidence confirming that the spouse can't be trusted. It's an insidious self-fulfilling prophecy of doubt and distrust.

In other words, you can't expect your spouse to make your fear go away. You have to make it go away. And you do that by taking an assertive, not passive, posture toward your own fear.

Now, if a partner has earned your distrust through betrayal, you should step back and look for a change of heart on their part and evidence of changed behavior.[1] But that alone won't alleviate your fear. Only walking through your fear and, perhaps, experimenting with what it would be like to trust more of yourself to the other person will help you find out what's on the other side. You'll disprove your fear by forcing yourself to trust at a deeper level and making yourself vulnerable when you'd rather not. This is not easy. Take one small step at a time.

When your risk is met with the compassionate patience of a loving spouse, you'll share a new experience of safety as a couple. Each successive experience will soften your fear and move you toward each other. This below-the-surface security will then inform and broaden your above-the-surface money management options.

Sometimes when couples get stuck trying to settle a financial issue, both of them have below-the-surface issues that prevent them from finding a solution to the above-the-surface dilemma. However, we've also seen many situations where only one of them is insecure about the relationship while the other is focused entirely on above-the-surface logistics. For example, a parent might be focused on coordinating with a former spouse the payment of a fee for their child, but the stepparent is feeling left out and, therefore, threatened by the interaction between former spouses.

In any situation where there is a below-the-surface issue, seek to resolve that first, even if that means delaying a money management decision. The most important conversations you will have as a couple are around matters of commitment, companionship, and cherishing one another. In blended families, conversations may also need to address parenting and stepparenting priorities ("How can we be financial partners when you won't let me be a parental partner?"), coping with former spouses, and other stressful dynamics. Finding agreement about these matters while setting boundaries to protect and guard your family affirms your love for each other and raises confidence in the long-term dedication of each partner. When those below-the-surface insecurities are relieved, then return to above-the-surface financial decisions and find an agreeable solution.

With every step of this journey, each partner must act in a trustworthy manner. One man we'll call Justin insisted that his fiancée sign a prenuptial agreement before they married. Once they were married, he managed all of their finances and gave his wife access to only a monthly allowance. Seven years into their marriage, he set up a trust to provide for his kids and her as part of his estate, but he forced her to sign it without reading it or discussing the details. All of Justin's power plays and veils of secrecy inflamed his wife's trust issues. This is not how you do it. Instead, do everything you can to create an environment of transparency, compassion, patience, consideration, sacrifice, mutual risk taking, and trustworthy behavior.

If you can't resolve the underlying concerns by yourselves, we recommend seeing a qualified therapist as an investment in your usness.

When it comes to the day-to-day money matters, building equity in your usness means that, over time, you may evolve and revise your pot of money strategy—and a host of other money-related decisions—to match your growing sense of stability, safety, and oneness.

Stop and reflect. What are the below-the-surface issues in your relationship right now? Which of those are yours to manage and/ or change? Use the space below to summarize your thoughts.

_____

_____

_____

_____

_____

_____

Merging Logistics

Once below-the-surface issues are resolved, you will be in a better place to tackle the various above-the-surface logistics related to finances that need to be merged. Here are some best practices for merging with wisdom.

Bank Accounts and Holdings

Before you start discussing the logistics of merging bank accounts and holdings with your spouse, it might be helpful to share your banking history. How is it that you chose your bank or financial institution in the first place? Are there relationships you value there? Would merging accounts hinder or interfere with those relationships?

Names on accounts have legal and estate ramifications. For example, keeping certain assets individually titled may be the best option in some situations, especially if you have chosen the two-pot method of managing money, but keep in mind that this will affect how the accounts are directed in the event of death or disability. See chapter 11 for further details.

When it comes to bank accounts, there are four issues for a couple to consider:

1. *Who has current control and access to the funds?* Who can write checks, make deposits, or transfer money into or out of the account? Who will be responsible for paying bills from and managing a joint account?

2. *Who gets the account in the event of a death?* Do you intend for your spouse to have everything that's in an account if and when you pass away? Or is it your wish that some or all of a particular account goes to your children instead?

3. *How transparent are the financial transactions?* Even if your spouse is not named on an account, should you provide some way for them to see what's going on with it, through paper statements or online access? We've met with couples who express how well the three-pot system works for them, but in almost every case, they stress that everything that happens in every account is visible to both spouses. Finances can be both transparent and separate.

4. *How will money be deposited into the joint account?* You'll need an agreement about how much each person will put into the account, and how often (weekly, monthly,

or annually). Here are some examples we've heard of how blended families organize their three-pot system:

- Each spouse puts in 50 percent of the funds needed for shared household expenses. This is a good starting point for most conversations, because it seems fair, but what if you and your spouse have significantly different incomes or financial means? If putting in half of the needed funds every month takes a much larger percentage of one partner's income than the other's, they might be at a disadvantage.

- Each spouse adds to the pot based on their percentage of the family's total income. For instance, if one spouse earns $80,000 per year and the other earns $40,000 per year, then the spouse with two-thirds of the household income puts in two-thirds of the monthly household money.

- One spouse can offer to pay all the household expenses. Carl, a widower in his sixties, was engaged to Elaine, also in her sixties. Their finances were very different. Carl had a good retirement income and substantial investments. Elaine's income was from Social Security only, and her savings were modest. Because of the difference in finances, their Togetherness Agreement reflected Carl's willingness to pay all of the household expenses. They kept a three-pot system, but Carl planned to fund the entire third pot.

- Spouses come to an agreement that fits their unique circumstances regarding the household expenses, not based on assets or income. Marriage is about communication and compromise.

There are a variety of ways to set up the ownership of any account:

- *Individual Name.* This simplest and most direct title assigns every account to a specific person. This is often the option chosen by couples using the two-pot method of managing money. What are the pros and cons? An individual account can't be accessed by anyone else unless they are named as an agent under your durable power of attorney. An individual account is not subject to creditors or liabilities incurred by the other spouse. In the event of an account holder's death, no one, including the surviving spouse, will have immediate access to the funds. The account will be included in the estate of the account holder, and the value directed according to the will. The funds will be subject to probate along with any costs, public scrutiny, and possible delays that result from a contested will.

- *Joint Tenants with Rights of Survivorship (JTWROS).* Most often used by spouses, this joint ownership titling assures that the account is protected from probate in the event of a death and instead is immediately accessible to the other owner. Remember that if both names are on the account, it will pass to the joint owner, regardless of what the deceased spouse's trust or will says.

- *Tenants in Common.* With property owned as tenants in common, each person owns their percentage share of the account. At death, the will dictates what happens to that person's proportional interest. If there is no will, state laws apply. Tenants in Common is rarely used for bank accounts but is much more common in dealing with real estate.

Updating Beneficiary Designations

Tonya and Kevin were newly married and had six mostly grown children between them. They ran into issues when they started talking about life insurance. Tonya thought that a spouse should always be the primary beneficiary, and children should be secondary; Kevin believed Tonya and his kids should split the benefits fifty-fifty.

Below the surface, Tonya took his solution to be a statement of his priorities, believing that he was putting his children ahead of his commitment to his wife. Kevin was motivated by guilt over the pain his children felt during his divorce from their mother and the fear of not being able to provide for their college tuition.

As a couple, they needed to address their below-the-surface issues first before they could find an above-the-surface logistical answer to their insurance question. They sought the help of a marriage counselor, who helped them see that they shouldn't see the words *primary* and *secondary* as a statement of whom a partner loves most. This wasn't a competition. The real issue was about how to provide for the needs of both children and spouse.

Once Tonya and Kevin were on the same page emotionally, they could tackle the insurance question through the lens of their overall financial plans and goals. They discussed how much time they had for each of their goals, the amount of risk to their principal they were willing to take, and whether they had provision from other sources.

Different couples will have different answers to this question of insurance. For instance, if children don't have any other financial provision, you may decide to include them as partial primary beneficiaries with your spouse. However, if they have another source of financial provision in your estate, then you could decide that your spouse should be the 100 percent primary beneficiary of the policy, with the kids listed as contingent or second in line. Still another option, described in chapter 2, puts the life insurance proceeds into a trust that provides an income to the spouse during their lifetime and then to the kids after the spouse's death.

Managing Debt

Financial planners commonly recommend that families who are struggling with multiple debts utilize a snowball strategy. We agree. Here's how to do it: Make a list of all your debts and where the money is owed, and then organize it in order from the smallest amount to the largest. Make a concerted effort to pay off the smallest debt first, putting as much money toward it as possible, while making minimum payments on everything else. When the smallest debt is paid off, shift all the money you were paying on it each month to the next smallest debt, until it's paid off as well. Then apply the money from the first two debts to the third, and continue the process until all of the debts are paid. Snowballing the money means you can pay off large debts much more quickly when it is their turn.

While this is a familiar strategy in the financial advising world, the process might be complicated in a blended family, especially if one spouse has more debt than the other, or a different kind of debt that would soak up all of the funds at first. This may not feel fair. In fact, applying your money toward your partner's debt may bring up below-the-surface fears or concerns. Acknowledge these feelings and work through them together. Then implement the debt snowball strategy.

Investments

When it comes to investing, the very first question for a couple to answer is "What is the goal for this money?" That will determine how you invest, the risk you're willing to take, and the strategic framework you'll follow in implementing your investment plan. If your goal is to pay your child's college tuition and they're already a senior in high school, your investment strategy will be drastically different from how you plan for a retirement that's at least twenty years away.

It's also important to explore, as a couple, your investment risk profiles. That is, the longer you have to reach a goal, the more risk you can be willing to take regarding the erosion of your principal. But there's an emotional, below-the-surface layer to this as well.

Nick, for example, grew up hearing stories from his grandparents about the Great Depression. Their memories of losing all their money in the stock market, of being unemployed or under-employed, and how they scrimped and saved their way through the 1930s stuck with him. His father, who worked at a local bank, invested only in federally insured certificates of deposit or government treasury bonds; this further reinforced Nick's aversion to equity market investing. Nick avoided the stock market for years before he met Marilyn, investing only in CDs.

Marilyn, Nick's new wife, had a high risk tolerance. Her mother was a successful financial advisor at a prestigious brokerage firm, and she'd taught Marilyn that buying high-quality blue chip stocks, and then holding them for the long term, was the sure way to build wealth. It had worked for Marilyn's family.

As a couple, they explored their underlying assumptions and agreed that their widely contrasting perspectives on investment meant that they should stick to a two-pot method of investing, at least for now.

Another below-the-surface factor related to investing relates to grief and how it changes the way we treat money inherited from loved ones. George and Stacy had agreed to a very conservative risk profile for their retirement investments, with slow but stable bonds far outnumbering stocks subject to market fluctuations and loss. However, when George inherited his father's portfolio, he refused to sell any of the stocks. He felt that if 100 percent stock investment was good enough for his dad, it was good enough for him. He and Stacy agreed that this approach would pertain only to that specific pool of money inherited from his father.

Finally, as a couple you will need to agree on the financial advisors that you both trust. If you each had a financial advisor you trusted prior to your marriage, this may be a challenge. Here again, some couples opt for a two-pot system so that each spouse can continue to work with the professionals that they know and trust. Other couples may decide to go with the financial advisor to which one of them has become loyal, or to seek out an advisor who is new to both of them.

Real Estate

Real estate includes any property you own and may include your family residence, rental houses, business property, or farmland. Because of the high values of real estate, questions about ownership and financial responsibilities should be addressed in a Togetherness Agreement (see chapter 2) if possible.

When Lee and Mai got engaged, they began to discuss where to live. Each of them owned a house. Should they live in one house or the other, or sell both and buy a new home? There were plenty of below-the-surface issues related to the home for Lee and Mai, as there are for most couples. If they decided to move into one of the homes, it could lead to emotional friction, bringing up issues such as "I don't want to sleep in the same room her ex-husband used," or "If I move into his house, will he let me redecorate?"

Lee and Mai decided to sell both houses and buy another house. However, that led to another group of decisions. If they bought a house together and one spouse died, what would happen to the house? Would the surviving spouse's family get a share of the house?

1. *How do we pay for the house?* Like most couples in their situation, they had to agree whether one spouse would pay all of the down payment or they would split it somehow, and then how future mortgage payments would be handled.

2. *What happens to the house when one of us dies?* Like bank accounts, a house title can be owned through individual titling, joint tenancy with rights of survivorship, or tenants in common. A fourth option is for a house to be owned by a trust. If your intention is for the surviving spouse to keep the house no matter what, then a new house can be purchased as joint tenants with survivorship. Whoever lives longer will own the house outright and can continue to live in it, sell it and keep the money, or

leave it to whomever they choose on their death. On the other hand, if one spouse pays for the house and wants it to go to someone else of their choosing after the death of the surviving spouse, then a provision can be made in a trust to allow the surviving spouse to live there for their lifetime. After their death the house will go to the person designated by the original owner. (This will be explained in more detail in chapter 11.)

Businesses or Closely Held Corporations

What if one spouse owns their own business? Should you merge that in your marriage? In our experience, a business is the least likely asset to be merged in a blended family's day-to-day finances.

Here are a few issues to consider in thinking about business ownership:

1. Will both spouses work in the business or contribute funds to the business?
2. Do other family members work in the business? For instance, in rural communities where there are still lots of family-owned farms, two or three generations often work the farm together. The next generation's expectation is that the farm will be left to them to continue in the family business. Bringing a new spouse into the equation, especially one who is not active in farm management, can create concern. If the spouse inherits some or all of the farm, does that mean the other family members will lose their livelihood in addition to losing their loved one?
3. Does the spouse need income from the business for support if the business owner spouse dies? If so, some provisions could be made to provide for the spouse from the business income, whether or not the spouse will ever become an owner of the business.

Relational Trust

The most important thing in any financial decision is relational trust, which must be built before financial commitments can feel secure. We hope that you're in a better place now to recognize any below-the-surface emotional and relational issues that must be addressed so that you can consider the above-the-surface, practical matters of merging your financial lives.

And don't worry if you're not there yet. This all takes time. When stepfamily educators Gordon and Carri Taylor married in mid-life, they had an elaborate array of personal businesses, employees, financial obligations, adult and teenage children, retirement accounts, and investments. It was a lot to sort through, but they never felt disunified, because they made the decisions *together* about where they were headed. Together with their attorney, they devised a "trust-building agreement" (essentially a TA), which freed them to deal with their merging family relationships and strengthened their marriage as they watched each other honor the agreement.[2] Initially they thought the merging process might take years. But their relational trust and dedication to honoring the agreement made the process happen much more quickly.

4

Love and Boundaries

Kaelah and Stefan were in love, but trust was torn apart by their boundary problems. They each had two children and began their life together by selling each of their respective houses and buying a new one that they could all call home. But parenting disagreements (Stefan is a laid-back parent and Kaelah highly structured) and spending differences (Stefan is a spender who isn't afraid of credit cards or debt, and Kaelah is a saver who avoids debt at all costs) quickly led to division in their marriage. Stefan took his kids and left, moving into an apartment. After a few months, the couple began talking about getting back together. But how would they move forward?

The boundary around your yard or property defines your land from your neighbors' land. Boundaries marked on roadways define the rules for driving, space for your car, and, in the case of an accident, which driver is guilty of a violation, and, therefore, liable for the consequences.

Relational boundaries serve a similar function. They show belonging and loyalty (who's part of a family and what their obligations and responsibilities are), indicate the value placed on a given relationship (for example, the amount of time you devote to a relationship says a lot about how much it matters to you), and give definition to the rules of engagement between family members (Who is an authority to whom? What kind of touch communicates care, and under what circumstances? How do you show honor to others? When there is a disagreement, who makes the final decision and under what circumstances?). Furthermore, how you relate to each other within your marriage is a boundary matter, but marriage itself is an important boundary. With marriage, you acquire legal rights and obligations and expect sexual fidelity, financial provision and care, parental authority, and that you will give and receive preference to each other above all other relationships (including parents and children). That's why an affair hurts so much—it is a violation of the shared boundary of romantic and sexual fidelity. The broken trust results in feelings of betrayal, distress, and fear that the offending partner no longer prioritizes the marriage.

You need clear boundaries to know where you stand and how to move through life together. Kaelah and Stefan had strong feelings for each other, but they had not worked out the practical matters of being a family. When your boundaries are clearly defined and agreed on, and both partners honor them, each of you generally will feel safe, secure, and loved. If you have unhealthy boundaries, if one of you doesn't live up to your mutually accepted boundaries, or if you have unclear boundaries, you won't. For instance, if Alice believes she and her husband should pay the down payment for her adult child's first home, while her husband, Jim, doesn't, problems will arise both above and below the surface of the relationship. If Dan is fine with his twenty-six-year-old daughter moving back into the house after a messy breakup, but his wife, Carolyn, is not, there will be problems. Situations like these have multiple boundary components that need clarification and agreement, because ultimately these issues speak to matters of the heart: Do you love my child? Do you love *me*? I mean, *really* love me? Can I trust you to be there for me . . . for us? Below-the-surface matters are always the real issue.

Consider the following questions:

- Do you find yourself anxious when making a decision that involves your spouse and the children?
- Are you concerned about making someone angry with you or pushing people further apart from each other?
- Are you unsure of how to love your spouse well?
- Do you question their loyalty to you or feel insecure in your marriage?

The following boundary principles can strengthen your home even if you answered no to all four questions. If you answered yes to any of the above, then work toward the following healthy boundaries.

Striving for Unity

Finding and keeping unity in your marriage is a vital boundary to manage. But getting there can be challenging, because blended family couples have something working against them. Let us explain.

Every house has a foundation. Without it, the house couldn't withstand the weight of the structure or the seasonal and severe storms that batter it. Without a foundation, the walls and ceiling of the house would crumble.

Even though your relationship with your children preceded your stepfamily, your marriage is the foundation upon which the rest of your home is built. It is what the walls of your parenting stand on. It is what supports the covering of love that warms your children, gives meaning and purpose to family members, and protects everyone from the harsh elements of this world.

It makes sense, then, that when it comes to setting boundaries, your marital unity must be a priority. However, a blended family marriage is often fragile—especially during the early years of bringing together two family units—and is easily divided by issues of money and parenting. It is important, then, that you continually discuss what is happening in these areas and how it is taking place so you can strive for unity in how you will handle issues.

The first step is to decide the general process you'll use to negotiate important decisions. Agree to talk until you find unity, then implement the decision. This overarching boundary that prioritizes your couple unity will help you discuss specific boundary questions that arise. For example, after becoming a single parent, Miranda had to get used to making all the parenting decisions. When her husband entered the family, she had to change the boundaries around making parenting decisions again. She had to learn to slow down her decision-making and make room for him. If she had failed to include him, his role as stepdad likely would have been undermined.

Beyond prioritizing unity, try to anticipate and talk about needed boundaries before they arise. For example, if your children are adults, you'll need to anticipate expectations around the holidays, gift giving, your role as grandparents, and the like. If you still have children at home, boundary conversations will include parenting issues like behavior expectations in the home, media limits, preferred modes of punishment, and the values you want to teach your children.

You've probably already figured this out, but the "we all love each other, so it's all going to work out" approach just doesn't cut it in blended families—or any family, for that matter. Stepfamilies have so many moving parts, people, and priorities that it's easy to be blindsided by a situation and inadvertently find yourself on the opposite side of an issue from your spouse. So adopt an attitude that makes your couple unity a priority as you have continuous, proactive conversations around the boundaries in your family. This will give structure to the family and protect your marriage in the process.

Boundaries without Marriage

Perhaps it would be helpful to pause and add a comment here for couples who have chosen to live with a partner outside of marriage. According to a growing body of research, the overall level of commitment between partners who are living together without the permanence of marriage is typically lower than it is for married couples. On some level there is always the question "Are we really together or are we not?" Even when they have a child together, cohabiting couples are more likely to break up and not raise their child together, according to distinguished research professor Wendy Manning.[1] If that's true when they share biological children, how much less stable is a cohabiting stepfamily when a couple does not have a shared biological child? The relational boundaries in cohabitation are inherently ambiguous.

Even after living together for thirteen years, Karen and Stewart didn't know where they stood with each other regarding their financial futures. Agreements they made early on to share expenses ("I'll pay for this until you retire.") and provide for Karen's adult children and grandchildren weren't honored or became a source of contention. "Now he wants me to redo my will," she said, "but it seems lopsided. I have three people to worry about—him and my boys. He only thinks of himself."

Conversations with this couple revealed a common dynamic for couples living together: One partner has a higher level of commitment to the relationship and family than the other has. More often than not, it is the woman who has the higher level of commitment.[2] And she assumes her partner is more committed than he really is; that is, she assumes he is as committed as she is. She and her children are vulnerable because she thinks that her position in the relationship is solid, but in reality he's not all-in on their future. Children in cohabiting homes sometimes recognize this relational ambiguity and unequal commitment. This can result in a decrease in acceptance of the stepparent, respect for the stepparent, and sense of family permanence.

This is a serious issue—not just for financial stability but also for relational health. It's very difficult to set clear boundaries around parenting, money, couple unity, etc. when the foundation of the home has a huge crack in it. "Independent togetherness," as it has been called elsewhere, doesn't foster confidence, stability, or unity.[3] Walking around with a question mark above your head doesn't build trust or a sense of permanence. In our opinion, it is healthier to define a relationship as dating, and let your living arrangements reflect this, until you are ready for the full permanence of marriage.

Make Changes Together and Communicate Them Side by Side

Before marriage, the foundation of a single-parent home is the parent and their relationship with their children. After a wedding, a blended family establishes a new foundation around the married couple. This is a significant boundary shift that often results in changes to family rules and daily routines.

It is critical that you negotiate these changes together first and then communicate them in solidarity to your family. Again, this serves to protect and strengthen your marriage while empowering the stepparent as a part of the new parenting team.

Consider Sergio, for example. As a single dad he was always willing to hand money to his children whenever they asked. In effect, they decided when money was spent and what it would be spent on. This is a serious parental boundary problem. To be clear, Sergio's kids don't have a problem because they ask; Sergio does because he won't say no. (If you found an ATM with free money, wouldn't you go back for more?) Now, together with his wife, Sergio needs to define how much money is appropriate to give kids (his and theirs), as well as how often and under what circumstances to give them money. And then he needs to say no when the limit is reached.

But what if Sergio refuses to discuss the issue with his wife, or he agrees to set boundaries and then doesn't live up to them? Sergio's wife will reasonably assume that he is making a statement about what really matters to him: preserving the peace and satisfying his children's desires, even to the demise of his own personal finances and marriage. The parenting boundary problem that preceded Sergio's marriage is now a marital boundary problem that is sabotaging his relationship and his new family's ability to bond.

Let's consider another example that includes a former spouse. Victor is a successful businessman who regularly negotiates big financial deals. But ever since his divorce, he's catered to his ex-wife. In an effort to avoid conflict, he's agreed to give her more custody time and money than required by their divorce decree.

Then he married Felicia, a highly successful consultant who's not afraid of controversy. Victor and Felicia agreed that she would manage their finances. As soon as she looked at the books she told Victor's ex that they were no longer going to give her extra money every month. Felicia was simply trying to help her new family be better stewards of their money, and she believed setting limits would help Victor's children learn to do the same. The decision sent waves crashing through the co-parenting relationship, Victor and Felicia's marriage, and Felicia's relationship with her new stepchildren, who heard their mother's side of the story first.

The issue here, from our perspective, was not whether Victor and Felicia should reduce paying for things, but that Felicia acted without first discussing the situation with Victor. As a couple, they needed to decide how they would implement the changes. Surely, Felicia should have seen that there would be strong feelings about finances on both sides and many layers to consider. There would likely be numerous conversations before they could agree on what to do and find the courage and compassion to make the changes together. Whatever it took, finding unity would be well worth the effort because it would support their new, fragile marriage, their parenting and stepparenting, and the foundation of their home.

We should add this: Whether a matter is related to former spouses, children, or an extended family member, you can't always anticipate and prepare for the decisions that are going to throw a grenade into your living room. There are people and circumstances you can't control. Despite good intentions, mistakes do happen. But if you find yourself in a mess of intersecting boundaries, immediately pull back to regroup with your spouse, identify the below-the-surface issues that add fear and pain to the situation, and start talking about how to find unity. Then go back to anyone else in the family affected by the change and stand side by side as you tell them what to expect in the future.

Use Veto Power Sparingly

We want to caution you against a common mistake we see happen in blended families. All too often, when a couple struggles to agree on an issue relating to one spouse's children, the biological parent claims veto power and asserts a decision.

From a legal standpoint, it's true that biological parents have ultimate responsibility for their minor-age children, but unilaterally playing the "I'm the parent" card has a lot of negative consequences for your marriage and family. Instead, try to give mutual consideration and respect to each other's opinions and needs. At a minimum this means applying good communication and conflict resolution skills and trying to find the win-win solution.[4]

Twice, David and Mandy had adult children from their first marriages boomerang back into their home. Each time, they needed to decide how much financial help to provide. They talked and talked and talked and eventually made decisions they felt were appropriate for each child. In one case, Mandy's son had been irresponsible with money, and the couple decided not to help him with specific bills. He had to face the consequences of his poor choices. David's son, though, found himself in a situation that was beyond his control, so David and Mandy did provide financial support. In both cases, neither parent tried to dictate the decision just because it was their child. Different responses that potentially could have caused a divided home didn't, because the couple prioritized unity in their marriage, and no one asserted veto power over the other.

Consider the Parent-Child Relationship

Fear can sabotage a marriage and family. Fear is often the below-the-surface reason that biological parents try to dictate the boundaries of decision-making about their child. It might be fear that their child will suffer some disappointment, feel unloved, or experience some other emotional pain. It's also often fear that makes a stepparent try to alter the relationship between their spouse and their children.

Ann, who is in her midthirties, and her sister were happy for their dad, Ted, when he married ten years after their mother died. Ted had met a woman they liked, and given that both daughters lived a few hundred miles away from their father, they felt it was a godsend for him to have someone in his life. But soon after the wedding, Ann's stepmother, Barbara, started cutting them out of their father's life. She made excuses and other plans that kept him from seeing his daughters, even on Father's Day. When Ann and her sister drove three hundred miles to visit on another weekend, Barbara cut their time short by insisting that Ted fix something on her computer instead of spending time with his children. Barbara's behavior continued like this for years.

We don't know why Barbara acts the way she does, though experience suggests she may be fearful of not being first in her husband's heart. Whatever the cause, the unfortunate reality is that Ann and her sister have to deal with a possessive, divisive family member who violated the boundaries of the father-daughter relationship. Their father's passivity is not helping either. He could insist on connecting with his daughters and grandchildren. If Ted felt that Barbara's insecurities were affecting his ability to spend time with Ann, he should have spoken up about that. Sure, doing so would likely result in a conflict between him and his wife, but that conflict might force them to deal with their current pattern of unhealthy boundaries. If he doesn't speak up, and that pattern continues, it could destroy this family.

Let's pause and look at the two dynamics that are unhealthy here: Ted is avoiding conflict, and Barbara is making unilateral decisions and actions.

Sometimes relationship boundaries between biological parents and their children need to change. Especially after a loss, the bond between a single parent and a child that was initially helpful during a season of pain can be so close it isolates them from everyone else. But changes to that relationship should never be due to a one-sided or manipulative endeavor by a stepparent.

Distinguished family therapist Edwin Friedman writes that many so-called wicked stepmothers are just women who take too much responsibility for changing an irresponsible child or their husband's relationship with his child.[5] Did you catch that? Taking responsibility to change a parent-child relationship is the issue.

Perhaps Barbara saw that Ann and her sister were enmeshed with their father and needed to grow up a little and focus more on their own families. Or perhaps Ted kept bailing Ann out financially, and it was taking them both under. Barbara's actions might not have been completely selfish, as we assumed at first. Nevertheless, she shouldn't have taken this action unilaterally. Barbara should have consulted with her husband and sought a respectful, loving solution in unity with him. Perhaps they could agree to make some adjustments in how they share their time (sacrifices will likely have to be made on both sides, but it would be something worked out together).

Then, if the decision they agree to has implications for Ted's relationship with his children, *he* should speak to Ann and her sister about it. Why him? Because blood talks to blood, especially when the blood relationship is affected by the decision. This likely would be very difficult for Ted to follow through on given his history of avoiding controversy and being passive. This would be his growing moment too.

Even if Ted and Barbara find unity in the new boundaries they want to set, will the changes still bring about some anxiety and conflict between the various family members? Will there be tension in the communication and implementation of the decision? Will apologies have to be made and forgiveness granted? Most certainly. And adjustments to the new boundaries might have to be made along the way, but with care, both Barbara and Ted's unity and the father-daughter relationship will remain.

Defining ambiguous boundaries is not easy. Sacrifices will be made, people will feel anxious and uncertain, and hard decisions to support your marriage will be made. However, the end result—a stronger family—makes the gain worth the pain.

5

Money and Former Spouses

magine that you're boarding a plane, headed home after a few days away. As everyone is getting situated, the man directly behind you is having a conversation on his phone. A rather *loud* conversation. There's no way not to overhear his half of the dialogue.

"No, honey, I'm not. I do not care for—" The man is clearly interrupted. Then, "I am not bowing down to her."

A pause. And then, "Oh, honey, I can't change the court order. You know I can't change it."

Another pause. "It's bothering you, and I have no idea why. I don't understand."

He listens. "Sweetie, that alimony has nothing to do with us."

The next time he speaks, he's louder. "What? You've known me for seven years. I've never had anything to do with my ex-wife."

Whatever she says in response draws a sarcastic reply. "Really? I'm sorry you feel that way. I'm *really* sorry you feel that way."

Then he tries to console her. "I don't love her, sweetie. . . ." There's another pause. "Why are you getting this way? Would you please calm down?"

"No, I didn't." His voice is definitely raised now. "Sweetie, when you scream I cannot hear what you're saying."

He listens for a few seconds but sounds angry when he answers. "Okay, fine. You're 'done with it.' Tell me what that means."

"Now stop it," he snaps. "We've had this conversation before. It wasn't my decision. In a few years I won't have this obligation anymore. Do you think I would pay her if I didn't have to?" He pauses. "What? I wouldn't."

"That didn't have anything to do with your bills. Only mine." Another pause.

"Well, I hope we figure it out soon," he snaps, and then you hear the sound of his phone being slapped onto the tray table, the conversation clearly over for now.

So what do you think are the below-the-surface issues here? Without context it is hard to know exactly. Perhaps his wife (or girlfriend) is greedy, or maybe she's fearful that he's still in love with his ex-wife. Maybe he's let his boundaries slip, and the continued financial tie to his ex has become a problem. Maybe the woman on the phone is concerned about the needs of their children. Maybe it is something else entirely—or all of the above. There's no way of knowing for sure.

The more important point is this: Emotionally, financially, and relationally, the past is never fully out of the present. Managing the relationship with your former spouse, especially if they are the parent of your child, is part of financing your togetherness. You may not have this same conversation, but you will have boundary conversations.

The principles based on love and boundaries we offered in the previous chapter for parenting and money issues apply to former spouses as well. Prioritize your marriage and seek unity in how you deal with former spouses. In addition, these co-parenting practices and attitudes will be helpful.

Helpful Co-Parenting Practices and Attitudes

The Smart Stepfamily discusses in great detail the challenges of relationships with former spouses and what healthy co-parenting looks like. You can find much more on the subject there. But for this book, suffice it to say that typical below-the-surface issues between former spouses include hurt, animosity, bitterness, resentment, and distrust.

Further, any negative emotional residue left over from the breakup can plague a co-parenting relationship well after a divorce. The negativity can spill over onto your above-the-surface parent-child relationships, your co-parenting money matters, and even your blended family marriage.

Martin's former wife, for example, was bitter about their divorce. She manipulated their children, cut into Martin's visitation time, and did not carry her weight when it came to paying for things. Martin's current wife, Camille, was angry at the ex and at Martin for being too passive in his dealings with her. Martin tried to tell her that he didn't put his foot down with his ex because he wanted to protect his kids from conflict. Things would get worse for them, he believed, if he held his former wife accountable. But as the financial burden began to rise, so did the conflict between Martin and Camille. When Martin's oldest daughter went to college, his former wife missed her part of the payments, forcing Martin and Camille to take on the entire cost. Yet she still occasionally blocked his visitations with his younger kids.

Act Divorced

We suspect that Martin's former wife is refusing to "act divorced," that is, fully accept being divorced. In many cases, partners keep acting married long after a legal decree ends the marriage. Emotional and psychological dissolution is slow.

A partner who feels they still need to make their former spouse suffer is still acting married. They haven't separated their emotional well-being from their ex-spouse's, and they remain so painfully tied to their past that they think that expressing anger and making the other hurt will somehow make themselves feel better.

We intertwine ourselves with the person we marry, both emotionally and psychologically, but a key part of divorce is undoing this. The process of *de*-coupling is difficult and painful, but it needs to be done, especially if either of you is moving forward into a new relationship and a blended family.

Why? Because you can't think objectively about your co-parent exchanges, or use common sense in your necessary communication, unless you do. Ask divorced parents what it means to act in the best interests of their child, and most will say that parents should cooperate with their child's other parent. But when they are still emotionally tied to their former spouse, those best interests fall to the wayside. They still blame the other for their own issues, and they hold on to bitterness over the failed marriage.

Worst of all, they still try to get out of their former spouse what they could never get out of them in the marriage.

That's not good for anyone. If you've been through a painful divorce, stop and evaluate your heart to make sure that you've fully let the marriage go. Unhook emotionally from your former marriage. It's the only way to take your life in the present back.

Forgive

Harboring bitterness and pain below the surface will sabotage healthy co-parenting. Finding the willingness to forgive your former spouse will set you free.

Perhaps it's good to discern what forgiveness is not.

Forgiving is not minimizing how your former spouse hurt you; if anything, it properly acknowledges the seriousness of offenses but lets them go anyway.

Forgiveness is not being passive in the face of an offender. It's actively choosing to no longer be their victim.

And forgiveness is not making yourself vulnerable to someone who can't be trusted. Trust and forgiveness are two different things. Forgiveness means letting go of an offense; trust means viewing someone as trustworthy. You can forgive a former spouse and not trust them. In fact, we would suggest that's just what is needed in situations where an ex has repeatedly proven themselves unreliable. Forgive them to let go of your bitterness, but don't trust them beyond what they earn. Don't unnecessarily expose yourself and your kids to being hurt by them. Finding the balance is not easy, but releasing yourself from the hurt of the past will empower you to act divorced and manage your below-the-surface issues more effectively so you can become a more effective co-parent.

It's All about the Kids

You've probably heard the co-parent mantra "It's all about the kids." Between-home negotiations are not about you and your needs, or about your relationship and history with your ex. Co-parenting is about both parents prioritizing the needs of the children, including financial needs. When parents forget this, kids are exposed to conflicts over money as well as other issues.

When former spouses bicker over little details or nickel-and-dime each other, they make the situation about themselves, not the children. That undermines the basic mutual respect each home needs to have for the other in order for co-parenting to run relatively smoothly. And when one parent fails to honor their part of the financial care for the children, it often sabotages everything: between-home finances, the broader level of co-parenting cooperation, even the parent's relationship with their children. Kids resent it tremendously when a parent fails to pay their child support and/or alimony, because that reduces the child's opportunities in life and adds hardship to their living conditions.

All you accomplish by not doing your part is generating resentment toward yourself. You might feel your kids distancing themselves from you as well. Effective co-parenting, then, begins with a commitment to pull your weight and bring a good attitude to every money conversation.

Remember the man on the plane who was talking loudly on the phone? He shared his negative comments about his ex-wife with everyone within five rows of him. What do you think the odds are he also shares his negative thoughts in front of his children? Pretty high, actually. And that's a problem.

The research on what hurts children after divorce is clear: High levels of parental conflict before, during, and after divorce harm their well-being (no matter their age). When former spouses contain their conflict (keeping it low and not exposing children to it), don't force children's loyalties, and act as authoritative parents, kids fare better, says psychologist Robert Emery in his book *Two Homes, One Childhood*.[1] So, make co-parent cooperation a high priority.

When Co-Parent Conflicts Occur

When you can't prevent conflict, try to manage it. Research has identified ways to reduce the negative impact of parental conflict on kids.[2]

- Don't fight about the kids.
- Don't fight in front of the kids or privately criticize your ex to them.
- Reduce the intensity of your expressed anger (be luke-warm or cooler).
- Don't let your conflict become physical.
- Do not expect or ask kids (even in private) to take a side or get in the mix.
- Resolve the conflict, even if you just agree to disagree.

One good attitude to adopt is to "aim for general fairness, not down-to-the-last-penny fairness," says a *U.S. News & World Report* article citing author Kimberly King.[3] A tight, legalistic attitude doesn't have grace and doesn't invite a spirit of collaboration from the other parent. Yes, this may mean compromise, or even paying more at times than what you're legally required to, but focusing on the goal—your child's provision and care (and sometimes wants)—will make the sacrifice worth it.

Let's look at a real-world example. Kathy's ex-husband was behind on his child support. Kathy knew it was because he had lost his job due to the company downsizing and that he was trying to get back on his feet. He didn't have a pattern of nonpayment, and he had expressed to her how bad he felt about it. For the first few months, Kathy graciously pardoned the debt, but when friends and family told her she should find a way to squeeze it out of him, she started second-guessing herself. "Am I being a doormat?" she wondered.

We don't think so. It's the pattern that makes the distinction. If Kathy's ex had a pattern of nonpayment or poor financial decisions and she repeatedly rescued him, she would have a problem. But that wasn't the story here. They had both been generally fair for years, so Kathy's act of mercy at this point wasn't going to turn him into someone manipulative. It was a good way to keep a cooperative spirit between them.

Another co-parenting attitude for conflict that's worth its weight in gold is to be proactive in defining with your co-parent how you will settle financial dilemmas before they arise. This isn't about finding the solution to hypothetical problems; instead, it's about agreeing to a process that will guide you through problems if and when they arise.

For example, how will you deal with situations when one of you feels strongly that an expense is necessary and the other doesn't? One option would be to require whoever feels strongly in favor of the expense to foot the bill for all or most of it (at perhaps an eighty-twenty split). The parent who opts out in these cases should be required to explain to their child (if developmentally appropriate) why they're doing so. This caveat is about accountability, making sure that neither parent uses this to avoid financial commitment.

A second approach to this dilemma, suggested by Geoff Williams in his article "How to Split Parenting Expenses with Your

Ex," is to agree up front to handle disagreements the way most courts do. "Generally, if a court finds that expenses are reasonable and necessary, the cost is divided in proportion to the parents' income," says attorney Linda Kerns, as quoted in Williams's article.[4] If a mother makes double the income of her child's father, she is required to pay two-thirds of the expense, while he pays one-third. This system has a potential downside, in that the parent with the lower income could try to take advantage of the other parent by repeatedly suggesting additional expenses. Everything has a downside when dishonest, disrespectful people are part of a negotiation, which we'll talk more about in the following sections. The point here is that having a predetermined process, whatever it is, to guide you through dilemmas helps when those times come.

Before we move on, let's stop to acknowledge that you may feel frustrated after reading the previous section—and you might feel more frustrated after reading this section. It takes two willing parties to make these practices work. Not everyone is interested in striving to find what is generally fair or defining the process for how to settle financial dilemmas before they arise. Rare is the co-parent who looks beyond their personal history and puts on these attitudes and practices. *If we could be so cooperative and pleasant about tough things like this, we might still be married.* Exactly.

And yet most co-parenting relationships improve over time. That doesn't mean that yours will, and we can't say how long it will take for resentments to die down and old battles to fade into history. But generally speaking, co-parenting gets easier over time.

Your mission—should you choose to accept it—is to do your part, remain open to what God may do in the heart of your co-parent, and keep hoping things will get better. Until then, you may have to endure negative attitudes and behavior from your former spouse, which will make accomplishing anything in this chapter difficult. Don't despair, and don't underestimate the strength you have to bring about positive changes over time. Your power is in managing your boundaries, your choices, your actions.

Dilemmas in Parenting with Former Spouses

Here are some common situations that we've seen blended families face. This might help you identify the places where you need to negotiate a process with an ex ahead of time, or at least help you through should the issue arise.

They Don't Use Child Support Like You Wish

If your responsibility is to pay court-ordered child support, what can you do if your ex isn't spending it the way you'd prefer?

Like many matters between former spouses, the first step is to understand how extreme the other parent's behavior is. A child who is not being fed, clothed, or given basic material needs is in an extreme situation. In such a case, the authorities should be contacted and action taken to ensure your child's safety. These situations are black-and-white.

Most other situations, though, are gray. Custodial parents, the law presumes, provide food, clothing, and housing for their children; noncustodial parents contribute financially to these costs. As long as the child's physical needs are being met, judges are generally slow to get involved. Even if you suspect the other parent is spending some of your money on themselves, the court likely will not take action unless the child's needs are ignored or neglected.

It's important to remember that there are many expenses in raising a child beyond the basic needs, and child support can be used for them. A custodial parent does not have to account for how their child support is being used. So, barring extreme circumstances, we suggest you not try to dictate, or even influence, the specifics of how child support is spent unless there's good reason to speak into an expenditure.

In fact, trying to influence how another adult, even a co-parent, spends their money says a lot about your desire to control the situation, and it's likely to sustain or increase conflict between you and your former spouse. What they do with the money is up to them; unless your child is in jeopardy, stay out of it.

A Parent Who Won't Pay Child Support

There are many reasons why parents do not pay their child support as required. Some are irrational (like thinking their children are better off without their presence), some selfish (arguing that they didn't want to be a parent in the first place), and others quite understandable (like the loss of a job). But all are violations of a court order and should be taken seriously, especially as it relates to the care of a child.

Earlier we told you about Kathy, whose former spouse had fallen on hard times and wasn't able to pay his child support. He had a track record of caring for his children and being responsible about making his payments. Kathy's ex is a good example of why it's important to consider each story individually, so as not to be punitive or condemning. You can tell when someone's heart is in the right place but life has made it difficult for them to follow through.

But what about when a former spouse's pattern is irresponsible and neglectful behavior? How should you respond then?

Unless this situation is extremely new, you probably have already tried a number of things to get them motivated and activated. If and when these efforts fail, you may start asking if you should take your child's co-parent to court.

Sometimes this is necessary, but the thing to consider here is leverage. How do you most effectively motivate someone who isn't motivated to fulfill their obligations? When all else fails, filing for contempt of court is likely the best option, because courts have leverage you don't have. A parent in violation of child support faces fines, payment of all attorney fees, and in extreme situations, even jail time. No one hopes it will come to that, of course, but the threat of such things may help your ex find much-needed motivation.

On the other hand, going back to court may result in other costs to you. It may further antagonize your co-parent or the children or bring about protest behavior from extended family or the children

88

("Why are you doing this to Mom?"). Talk to your lawyer, weigh the possible reactions on all sides, and pray over your decision. Weigh each of those possible reactions carefully before moving forward, understanding that you probably can't find a solution that will satisfy every concern. You will likely second-guess yourself constantly. This often paralyzes parents, resulting in inaction that allows things to progress from bad to worse.

Modifying Child Support

There are legitimate reasons to change a child support order, and either parent may formally ask the court to consider doing so. Typically, this happens when changing circumstances for either parent or the child (for example, a decrease in income or a child's disability) prompt a request to increase or decrease the payment. Conflict can ensue if the two sides don't agree on the precipitating circumstances or what the changes should be.

Again, whether or not conflict arises is one consideration, but not the only one. If there are legitimate reasons for the change related to the child's well-being, it's important for everyone involved to be open to exploring the possibilities.

If you negotiate a temporary change to child support, be careful not to make only verbal agreements. It is best to get changes in writing. Imagine a former husband and wife who decide to lower the monthly payment due to the father's temporary layoff. "Just pay half for now," she says. A few months later, when his work hours return to full-time, she asks when he plans to catch up on the missing funds from the previous months. He didn't think he would have to make those payments up, and she assumed he would when he could. The spirit of cooperation in these co-parents was commendable, but the vagueness of their agreement—and the lack of legal standing—could turn their well-intentioned misunderstanding into a huge argument and legal battle. Get changes in writing and have a judge sign a court order based on the agreement.

A Marriage Caught in the Cross Fire

Co-parenting matters also involve your marriage. Kami and Jerome argued over the fair use of his income. Jerome had two children in his first marriage, and the couple had one son together. Kami struggled with how much of Jerome's income went to child support for his kids, leaving what felt like not enough for their child.

"It's not fair," she would say. "I want all of his kids to be provided for. Why should my son get the short end of the stick? Jerome needs to go back to court and get the amount reduced, but he refuses. It's just not right."

Kami is a mother looking out for her son. Whether Jerome's child support amount is fair is for the court to decide, and they might need an attorney who can help them determine if a reduction is in order. What's important for the marriage, though, is to guard against us-versus-them language about the children. This dynamic polarizes Kami and Jerome as a couple; she aligns with her son, and he aligns with his other two children, leaving the couple pitted against each other. The outcome is a divided household.

In some cases, a stepparent may have to accept their spouse's financial obligations and live with the ramifications. In other cases, a biological parent may need to go through the hassle of renegotiating alimony and/or child support. However, the ultimate cost to avoid is a divided marriage and stepfamily. That cost is far too high.

Unilateral Expense Decisions

Child support is designed to contribute to the basic costs of raising a child. Expenses like housing, food, clothing, health insurance, and medical bills are straightforward expectations. What's unclear, however, is how to handle expenses like extracurricular activities, traveling sport teams, private school, and even college tuition. The conflict escalates when one home considers an expense necessary while the other does not, or when one home unilaterally makes decisions that commit or attempt to commit the other home to participate.

Hopefully your custody agreement or negotiated parenting plan has a clause that specifies how much each household will pay for these kinds of expenses (for example, a fifty-fifty split, or an amount proportional to each parent's income). If not, a mediator may be needed to help you negotiate the rules going forward.

In any case, a good principle here is one that we've already explored: Don't make unilateral decisions and expect the other parent to pay up. Instead, approach the other parent and let them be part of the discussion and decision about the expense. Robert Emery says that an agreed-upon goal to bless the child with equal parental input makes it far more likely that both parents will agree on the expenses and be happy with the outcome.[5]

Should Your Current Spouse Get into the Negotiation Mix?

This is a common question for blended families who experience mid- to high-conflict co-parenting situations. (Low-conflict co-parents are generally able to talk through parenting and money issues without too much difficulty.)

Ideally, the biological parents work together for their children. But we understand that negotiating is difficult, if not downright challenging, when the former partners have so much negative history. You may be unable to separate what's personal from the parental responsibilities at hand, and so the question arises whether a stepparent should step in and negotiate on behalf of their household.

Every situation is different, and that's why we don't think there's a right answer to this question. If the stepparent is willing to be involved and they have the temperament of a mediator or peacemaker, give it a try. For example, if a stepdad and biological dad can have a productive discussion about between-home parenting and money matters, then the biological mom doesn't have to take part in the conversation.

Some stepfamilies find that this is a temporary arrangement that helps everyone through a challenging season, and others find it is a good long-term solution. In any case, it is important for the stepparent couple to talk a great deal in advance of the negotiation so the stepparent can represent their household well when talking with the other home. Once the conversation with the other home begins, the stepparent should not make any commitments before talking again with their spouse in private unless they are completely confident they know the biological parent will be okay with the decision.

Communication Strategies That Help

Sometimes the outcome of a money or boundary conversation depends largely on how you start it. Having a business mentality in your parental exchanges can be helpful. Good principles for having effective co-parent meetings include the following:

- Pick a time that is convenient for both of you. In our experience, meetings just before or after visitation pickup or drop off are not a good idea, mostly because the kids are present. Talk another time.
- Keep discussions brief and focused on the children (or parental decisions), and be polite and respectful.[6]
- Address schedules, academic reports, behavioral training, and spiritual development. Do not discuss your personal life or theirs. If the conversation turns away from the children, simply redirect the topic or politely end the meeting.
- If you cannot talk with your ex face-to-face due to conflict, use email, text, or voice mail. Do what you can to make your meetings productive for the children.[7]

Assuming your parental business meetings follow these guidelines in general, keep these specific principles in mind when engaging in a conversation about money.[8]

Open with an Invitation, Not a Demand

Instead of saying, "I need more money today to cover this," say, "Ella's travel team is adding games, and they're farther away. It's getting expensive. Could we meet to discuss her plans?" You've had time to consider the situation and arrive at the conclusion that more financial support is required; give the other person the chance to do the same. If you just declare what needs to happen, you can create a control issue. Give the co-parent a chance to think about it and process the information. At that point, a collaborative decision to contribute money is more likely.

Open with a Question

"Dillon wants a tutor. How do you feel about that?" Starting the conversation like this respects the other parent's opinions and gives them a chance to process the situation. Again, you've had a chance to do that, so make sure they get to as well.

Show Gratitude

Whenever possible, begin the conversation with gratefulness for what your co-parent has already done before discussing additional expenses. "I appreciate you paying for the band fee and instrument rental. I've paid for the uniform and competition travel costs as agreed. But now the school is asking we pay for the hotel at the competition." Asking for more without acknowledging what both parties have already done feels cold and is likely to make your co-parent feel taken for granted. Keeping your heart appreciative makes openness from them more likely.

"You go first. What do you think is fair?"

Especially if there is friction between you, this approach changes the dynamic from one of you trying to be in control of the solution ("Here's what should happen") to one where the other can take the lead and be responsible for finding what's fair. Of course, there's no guarantee their opinion will match yours, but it might at least shift the climate of the dialogue away from power and control to collaboration.

Final Thoughts

Sometimes former spouses and new stepparents assume that because a couple is no longer married, they won't have below-the-surface relational issues to deal with. Nothing could be further from the truth.

As in all relationships, it's vital to know what your personal hot buttons are, why you react the way you do with a co-parent, and how you can regulate your emotions in the midst of tension.

Divorces and nonmarital breakups tempt people into viewing the other person as the bad guy and themselves as the victim. This false narrative can leave you blind to any contributions you may bring to ongoing conflict; it's easy to blame the other person and focus on their faults and totally miss your own. Managing money with former spouses starts when you look closely in the mirror.

6

Computers, Cars, and Cash

The conversation started, as it usually did, in the car. "Dad, I need a phone."

Jack stifled a sigh. His daughter Abby was only ten, but they'd had this conversation many times over the past few months, usually as Jack was driving Abby to her mom's. He'd been noncommittal, not wanting to start an argument right before he dropped her off for another week apart, but he believed she was way too young for a phone.

"Daaad," Abby persisted. "If I had a phone, I could call you whenever I want. And what if I need something? Remember that time last year when Mom forgot to pick me up at soccer, and I was stuck there for an hour because the coach didn't have your phone number? If I had my own phone, that wouldn't happen."

It was a good argument, Jack thought, and he felt himself start to cave. Maybe a phone was important for her safety.

But then the flood of questions hit him. Would he pay for Abby's phone, or should her mother? Who would pay for the monthly service plan? This kind of thing wasn't covered in the divorce agreement they'd made when Abby was still a toddler. And what would Jen, his wife, say? She'd been adamant that the kids from her first marriage not get phones until they started high school.

For that matter, what would Abby's mother say? He had no idea how his former wife felt about Abby having a cell phone.

But he couldn't just keep ignoring his daughter's request either. "Okay," he said, "I'll talk to your mom and to Jen, and sometime before your birthday we'll come up with an answer about when and how you'll get a phone."

Abby sank back into her seat, mollified for the moment.

Sound familiar? Growing and thriving in your blended family isn't just about taking care of the big-ticket items like retirement and estate plans. It's also about navigating the daily financial decisions that come with a growing family.

Computers, cars, and cash—those are the most consistent areas parents must navigate, but they're also just the beginning. Families today face an unending stream of expenses and decisions.

- Laela's stepsons, twelve and fourteen, both want to try out for traveling sports teams this year. But between league fees, travel, and lodging for weekend tournaments, a single baseball season could cost the family more than $10,000. That would stretch their budget to the breaking point. And what about activities for Laela's six-year-old daughter? How will they be equally generous with her?

- Amir and Marta's oldest daughter, fifteen, will get her driver's license in a few months. But what will she drive? Should Amir and Marta buy her a car? If so, what kind of precedent will that set for their four younger kids, two of whom live mostly with their father, who likely will not buy them cars? Will they have to buy five cars? Will it create conflict between homes?

- Tasha's two teenage stepchildren arrive at her house every other weekend flashing top-of-the-line tablets and computers. Her own elementary-school-age kids are already pressuring her to buy them gadgets like their siblings have.

But Tasha doesn't want to spend money on state-of-the-art portable electronics for kids who still lose their coats and shoes on a weekly basis.

The questions just keep coming.

Sometimes, the decisions are easy. But for many couples, especially those in blended families, the regular expenses are minefields, creating conflict and division with your child's other parent, your kids, and your stepkids, and sometimes in your marriage. And as always, there are above-the-surface and below-the-surface issues involved in each.

You don't have to let your situations—or your credit card bill—create havoc in your life. With some careful planning and discussion, your family can approach financial decisions calmly and rationally, with a set of guiding principles that will help you navigate most of the situations your kids throw at you.

Like with most things in parenting, one solution does not fit all. Couples have adopted as many different approaches and philosophies to managing expenses as there are combinations of family blending. The successful, happy ones, though, all have a few things in common: ongoing communication, an adherence to agreed-upon principles, a willingness to be flexible, and a commitment to review and make adjustments as needed.

Throw Away That Idea of Being Equal

How many times have you heard a parent say, "We treat all of our kids equally?" Perhaps you've even said something like it yourself.

Equal treatment is a worthy goal, especially in blended families. As parents, we want to eliminate the sense that we are playing favorites. However, when it comes to financial decisions, treating kids equally ignores a variety of realities:

Each child is different. They have different skills, different passions, and different challenges. Your investment in sports for one child may help them develop a lifelong passion (and get a college scholarship), while for another sports would be just a passing interest. Buying a state-of-the-art computer for a child who spends their time programming and learning software design isn't the same as buying one for a child who mostly uses it to chat with friends on social media.

Children mature at different rates. If you assign specific ages to your decisions ("We will buy each child a cell phone when they turn thirteen."), you limit your ability to be flexible according to each child's unique development.

Your situation changes over time. Perhaps when your oldest child was born a decade or more ago, you couldn't afford many material gifts, but now you're more established in your career and there's more money in the bank account for luxuries. Or maybe it's the other way around; perhaps you had more resources when you only had one child, but now things are stretched thin. Your decisions must line up with the reality of your bank account first, even if that means that your kids don't all get exactly the same benefits. Your financial decisions can't happen in a vacuum.

There are other people in your children's lives. Your child's other parent, various grandparents, and even friends can affect the equality factor in a blended family. Some grandparents give significant gifts to their biological grandchildren and not their stepgrandchildren. And your child's other parent, if they're involved, might pay for things that their stepsiblings don't have. If your ex runs a car dealership and is able to give each of his children a car when they turn sixteen, that changes the equality equation.

Equality isn't possible, but being equitable is. Equitable means being impartial and just, honoring each member of the family and meeting their specific needs in the best way possible at a given time. As you and your spouse approach financial decisions, your priority should be to consider what is equitable in a situation.

Tim's family is a good example. He has five children in his blended family. For four of them, he and his wife navigated the purchase of phones and gadgets and cars and stays at overnight camp. But one of his daughters from his first marriage was born with special needs. She'll never drive a car or live independently. She has no use for a computer or a smartphone. She has no interest in the latest trends or nicest clothes.

What Tim's daughter needs, even now that she's an adult, is for Tim to visit her regularly and spend time with her one-on-one. For years, that meant a five-hour-each-way drive and an overnight hotel stay. Those travel expenses added up, but they were an equitable cost. Tim's daughter doesn't need money; she needs her father to be present in her life and manage her care. And she will need that for the rest of her life, even as Tim's other children grow to adulthood and start taking over their own expenses.

As a Couple, Talk Early and Often

Throughout this book we've encouraged you to consider communication to be your first and best financial planning tool, and these day-to-day situations are no different.

Don't wait until your daughter tells you she needs a check for a year of judo *today*, or until your oldest child is standing in front of you, driver's license in hand, before you start to consider how to handle these situations.

As a couple, sit down regularly to discuss any upcoming, predictable expenses for your children. Put this discussion on the calendar.

One good trigger is a child's birthday. Two or three months before each child passes their next milestone, set aside time with your spouse to consider what your child is likely to need in the next year and how you'll handle those needs. (If you can include the child's other parent in this conversation, do so. You'll be able to present and enforce a united decision. But if that's not possible in your situation, don't skip the conversation. The priority is to come to a decision with your spouse.)

Ask yourselves the following:

What is the underlying purpose of each expense? How will it benefit my child and the family overall? Is this something essential? Is this a fun expense? Does it seem like it would develop into something valuable? A computer or tablet that's required by a school or special class might be considered essential, but a new game console is fun. A cell phone that a child can use to call or text home when they need to be picked up is a practical expense, but perhaps the top-of-the-line smartphone with all the bells and whistles is not. Is a teenager's car a reward for growing up or a practical benefit that relieves some of the pressure of car pools and after-school pickups?

Are there special circumstances or concerns for this individual child? Just because your oldest child couldn't handle a cell phone responsibly at fourteen doesn't mean that her younger brother would act the same. As a couple, discuss how a new expense, purchase, or responsibility would benefit this specific child. If there's something they're excited about, even if you have doubts, discuss whether you should let them try. Or you may want to put additional limitations on a child who hasn't yet shown an ability to make responsible choices.

Why do I think what I do about this expense? Why does my spouse have their opinion? Step back from your initial responses to understand what's driving them. Is your concern or enthusiasm based on your own upbringing or on the advice of someone you trust? Perhaps you think that your child should work and save money to buy their own car, because that's what you did. Or perhaps your spouse is hesitant to give your middle schoolers a new computer because of all the things that they might be exposed to. Our parental philosophies and approaches develop over time. Stepping away from the immediate situation and talking together about where your attitudes and ideas come from helps you both understand the underlying motivations and parental goals that you each bring.

As much as possible, use these questions and this discussion as a chance to focus on your child's needs and to support and motivate them. Also be aware that at some point, a separate, messy slew of below-the-surface emotions or perspectives may try to derail you. Here are some examples:

> *I feel guilty for not being a bigger part of her life, so I'll buy her whatever she wants.*
>
> *His stepmother took him to that expensive concert, so now I have to take him somewhere even cooler.*
>
> *The kids have been hurt over the last few years with all the family changes. The least I can do is get them the things that make them happy now.*
>
> *Having a car will make up for the fact that his father is never around.*
>
> *All of her friends at school are trying out for the team. Am I holding her back from social development by saying no? Will she be treated like an outsider the way I was in school?*

Guilt, especially, is an emotion that works directly against the principle of being equitable. Guilt pushes us to spend more than we can afford and more than our children really need. It drives us to associate physical expenses with emotional healing. By talking with your spouse about your underlying assumptions and reasons for considering an expense, you have the chance to identify these lingering negative emotions and separate them from your decision. You can't undo the past, so focus on what's fair and best for your child now.

What can we afford? Often the decisions about what you can provide for your children will be practical as well as philosophical. You may want to pay for a family vacation to Disney World, but the bank account just doesn't have the funds right now.

It's okay to say, "I wish we could, but we can't afford this expense right now." Don't let yourself be pressured—by your child, your ex, or anyone else—into taking on expenses that you can't afford. It's more important for your child to learn responsible financial management and budgeting than to have the latest gadget or the trendiest clothes.

Make the Best Decision You Can

Before you make a decision, make sure you have the facts and a clear estimate of the real costs of any new activity or purchase. How much will your auto insurance go up if you add a teenage driver? If you sign up for a year of ballet, do you also need to buy shoes and costumes? How far will you have to drive to take your son to each practice? How much do games cost for the new console they're pestering you for?

Once you have all of the information, make a decision with your spouse (and your child's other parent, if possible) that you can all live with and enforce.

From the examples above:

- Jack and Jen, with Abby's mom's agreement, agreed that Abby was too young for a cell phone now, but in another year, when she entered middle school, they'd give her an inexpensive used phone to use for emergencies. If she handled that responsibly for a year (meaning she didn't lose it, didn't get in trouble for using it when she shouldn't, and didn't spend family time with her eyes glued to her screen), they'd give her an upgrade.

- Because both of the boys had been dedicated to baseball since their earliest Little League years, Laela and her husband agreed to give the traveling teams a one-year trial. They explained to both boys that they would have to forego their annual family vacation and cut back on Christmas presents. At the end of the year, they would revisit the subject and decide if the financial and time commitments were worth it. Their daughter, they agreed, was too young to show a specific interest in an activity. They

102

would continue to listen to her and respond if something came up.

- Amir and Marta agreed that it would be helpful for their oldest daughter to have her own car. They would give her their old, high-mileage hatchback for her sixteenth birthday, under the conditions that she pay for her own gas and spend a certain number of hours a week using the car to run family errands or otherwise help with chores. The couple would cover her car insurance for two years, until she turned eighteen, and then, if she paid the additional premiums, they'd keep her on the family's plan until she was twenty-two. Since Marta and Amir didn't have four more aging cars to give their other children, they established a "matching funds" plan: For every dollar their younger children saved in a "car" fund, Amir and Marta would match it. When each child earned their driver's license, they could use their money to buy whatever car they could afford. Marta and Amir tentatively agreed they would offer the same gas and insurance agreement but would revisit it after a few years to see if the system worked.

- Tasha and her husband agreed that they couldn't do anything about his kids showing up with their fancy phones and gadgets, but they did establish some boundaries for when all electronics needed to be put away. For now, there wasn't much else they could do. They would revisit specific decisions about what technology the younger kids could have in a couple of years. By that point, they said, laughing, they'd probably be talking about "smart pills" and implanted computers, not just tablets and fancy phones.

If You Disagree, Delay

Let's face it. You and your spouse aren't going to agree about everything in parenting. You each bring your own experiences, values, and personality. But that doesn't have to lead to conflict or hurt feelings. If you and your spouse are meeting and talking regularly about the expenses you can foresee, there should be enough time to let questions and decisions incubate.

If your husband thinks that your kids are ready for new smartphones, for example, but you're not so sure, agree to table the conversation for an agreed-upon period of time, like three or six months. Spend the time considering the decision, researching other options, watching your children, and considering your spouse's point of view. Are there less expensive, older models or effective parental controls that would make you more comfortable? Would the expense fit in the family budget? Is this a good investment?

It's important during this time not to let a disagreement about a specific decision poison the relationship. Let things incubate without animosity, knowing that you're both committed to doing what's best for your kids.

Come back together after the agreed-upon incubation time to share your perspectives again. This time, you need to make a decision. Don't keep putting things back in the incubator; a onetime delay isn't the same as continued inaction, and letting decisions slide indefinitely will inevitably hurt your child more.

If you find that you still can't agree, look for a compromise. If you have two separate decisions that need to be made, can you agree that one parent takes the lead and makes the decisions on one issue, and the other parent will handle the second?

For example, "Okay, if you're sure that this summer sports camp is important for Max, then let's go for it. Will you help him get registered? In the meantime, I'll make envelopes for the kids to save their allowances for back-to-school clothes and let them know that we'll match whatever they save to help them get a piece or two that they really want on top of the essentials that we provide."

As a family, you'll have plenty of these decisions to make and plenty of opportunities to discuss, decide, and compromise as a couple. Make sure that you're both listening and sharing and that one partner doesn't always "win." A mutual respect and willingness to trust the other person builds a deeper bond between you, and the practice of supporting each other creates a strong example for your children.

Communicate with Your Kids

Once you have agreed on a decision, share it and the reasons behind it with the child in question. Help them see why you came to the decision, rather than relying on "because I said so." If there are trade-offs or compromises that must be made, be clear about those as well. This encourages your child to be responsible about their decisions. If there are limits or stipulations on your agreement for you or your child, make sure to explain those clearly.

If your child's other parent wasn't involved in the initial discussion or decision, if possible, share your research, decision, and rationale with them as soon as you can. Do everything you can to present a united, respectful front to your child, so that they don't have the temptation to try to pit one parent against another.

And finally, be willing to revisit your principles and decisions for each child and each situation. The principle of "fair, not equal" means that you'll have a different set of factors to consider for each activity sign-up form, each new driver, and each request for a faster laptop. You'll probably disappoint someone at some point, but in the end, you'll have a family that's committed to growing and thriving together.

7

Parenting Adult Children and Caring for Aging Parents

When their youngest child left for college, Jon and Linda excitedly entered the empty nest season of their lives as a blended family. They anticipated that there would be adjustments and boundary issues to work out with their now-adult children, but they weren't prepared for how emotionally tiring it would be to figure it all out.

We never stop parenting our kids. Yes, our role shifts away from being an authority or director in their lives, but we never stop teaching, mentoring, and influencing their hearts and minds. But how do we do that without stepping on their toes? Without intruding on their personhood? Without violating their boundaries?

This challenge is compounded by the trend of boomerang children. In an article published by *Forbes*, Alan Dunn notes that "approximately 13% of adult children between 18 and 29 move back in with their parents after an attempt to live alone."[1] As young adults continue to struggle with unemployment and underemployment, many of them will bounce back into their parents' homes.

It's one thing to respect your child's boundaries when they are managing their own life, paying their own bills, and living in their own home, but how do things change when they step back into your home and need to rely on your provision? How do you let them be their own person when they aren't fully being their own person?

You can't dictate your child's behavior (they are an adult, remember), but you can be in charge of your resources and behavior, and bring a clear, unified approach to the situation. Defining relational and financial boundaries for these changing relationships is important for any parent, and creating a proactive financial plan is essential for stepfamily couples, because, as you will see, the above- and below-the-surface issues of a blended family can harm the couple's marriage.

Healthy Boundaries with Boomerang Kids

Before sharing two stories you can learn from, we want to outline some key principles for successfully navigating boomerang child scenarios.

First, just as we've encouraged you to do in previous chapters, make marital unity your number-one goal. Go out of your way to unite your expectations and proactively agree on how you will respond to situations that come up.

Do you remember David and Mandy from chapter 4? Two of their adult children moved back into their home unexpectedly, but neither boomerang situation divided them because they prioritized unity in their response.

Second, remember that past boundaries create an expectation for the present. If, for example, a parent always gave money to a child whenever they asked, that child will expect that same behavior as an adult, even if their parent has entered a new marriage. If the parent decides to respond differently now, they will have to overcome the inertia of the past. Making such changes takes courage. Keep these two thoughts in mind: Inertia is never a good reason for inaction, and change may be necessary in light of a parent's new commitments and the developmental needs of their family.

Third, be prepared for change. Anytime a child asks to return to your home, have a series of boundary-defining conversations both with your spouse and with your child to negotiate the nature of the relationships and expectations while the child is in your home. For example, you might need to explain to your child, "We want to respect you as an adult while you're here, and we understand that you are free to make choices. We can't tell you where to be all the time, but given our work schedules [or health matters], we ask that you be in at a decent time each night and that you not invite friends over if we're not here," or whatever you and your spouse have decided.

Those initial discussions should also cover the practical aspects of living arrangements and financial boundaries. For example, "I'm sure you'd like to help out around the house while you're here. What kinds of things would you like to do? Could you empty the dishwasher and take out the trash?" Or, in a situation where a child might not have a clear plan, "You're welcome to stay here for a few months, but you need to pay rent and help make dinner sometimes—and we'd like to see your business plan for moving out on your own. That's your goal, right?"

Keep in mind that all of the above boundaries already have expectations (both yours and theirs) attached and, therefore, have an inertia based on past family behavior. But your relationships are constantly changing, and what often takes both parents and children in a blended family by surprise is how what used to feel comfortable is no longer as easy because of the presence of the stepparent and perhaps stepsiblings. When a family changes, so does what makes sense or seems functional. As you will see in the following scenarios, boundary making in blended families can bring stress, even with adult children. Applying the principles above will certainly help.

"The Closer We Get to Marriage, the Closer I See Him Holding on to His Kids"

Diane and Richard, both empty nesters in their late fifties, had been dating for several years. Richard was a widower with two daughters in their mid-twenties, who had lived with him ever since they graduated from college. Diane was divorced, and her four kids, ages twenty-three to thirty, lived on their own.

Diane really loved and respected Richard, but she had concerns. "His kids are great," she told a close friend, "but he enables them. The closer we get to marriage, the closer I see him holding on to his kids. They continue to live in his home, expense-free and responsibility-free."

Diane and Richard had talked many times about their different viewpoints, but they hadn't been able to find unity about his daughters, and it affected their conversations about a possible marriage. Richard wanted Diane to sell her condo and move into his family home, but Diane wasn't comfortable living with his adult children, and she hesitated to sell her home.

"I believe he really loves me, but he won't risk making his kids uncomfortable or changing his expectations of them. It feels like he's forever going to be more concerned about their feelings than mine."

Let's apply the guiding principles discussed above to Diane's situation. It's clear that the couple is not unified in how they should respond to Richard's boomerang children. Some couples in their situation would be tempted to ignore the obvious disunity, thinking it will get better once they marry. In our experience, that's rarely the case. Thankfully, then, Diane is responding to the flashing yellow light in front of her and proceeding with caution.[2]

If this issue does not resolve, it may be a deal breaker for Richard and Diane. Richard's boundaries with his daughters have created their expectations for the present. If nothing changes and Diane moves in with them, she will find herself competing with their enmeshed relationship. Richard would be in the middle, and

110

given his history, likely side with his children despite his love for his wife. This would put the marriage in serious jeopardy.

It would be tempting for someone like Diane to try to coach Richard into treating his children like adults. But in reality, the change is not up to her. She can—and should—bring her concerns to his attention, but only he can orchestrate a change. If Diane takes too much initiative to motivate him toward this goal, he may end up resenting her—and his kids most certainly will.

Believing that "love will conquer all," many partners in Diane's shoes marry with the belief that their new spouse will make changes with their children after the wedding. Perhaps they even discuss the future and agree on what needs to happen. However, after the wedding the changes don't happen, or they come with a great price. That's why we feel strongly that the time to renegotiate boundaries with adult children is before a wedding.

Separating the change in parental boundaries from the establishment of a new marriage allows the biological parent to fully own the shift in their relationship. It's important for adult children to see their parent taking responsibility for any changes that happen. This makes the growth more permanent and means that if there is conflict, they can only blame their parent and not their new stepparent.

This is especially important because, in most cases, the change in parental boundaries needs to happen even if the couple never marries. Though the new marriage may prompt change, it's almost never the only reason for a change related to helping a parent let go. Helping adult children begin to act like adults is always the right developmental objective.

A Permissive Parent and Entitled Kids

Tony and Kaya have been married for two years. Her two kids are adults living on their own; one is in the military and another is in her senior year of college. Tony has five children from sixteen to twenty-eight. Like many blended family couples, Tony and Kaya have different parenting styles, and they raised their children very differently before their marriage. This has led to a number of conflicts.

Kaya grew up in a single-parent family without much money, and she started her first job at age fifteen. She helped her mother raise her younger siblings and financially contributed to the household budget while she was still in high school. As a divorced mom, she actively taught her kids money management and helped them save for college and live within their means.

"My kids made mistakes," she says, "but I didn't run to rescue them, and they learned from the consequences. Today, they're pretty savvy for their age."

By his own admission Tony and his first wife were permissive parents. They never expected much from their children or held them accountable for their decisions. Even now, Tony finances many of the activities of even his adult kids. His twenty-four-year-old is currently traveling the world with no goal for the future, and his twenty-six- and twenty-eight-year-olds are living with him and Kaya. The most recent marital conflict came when Tony gave one of them cash to go on a date.

The contrast between these two parents' boundaries and expectations couldn't be more pronounced. And, as you can imagine, these differences dramatically impact the step-relationships within the home. Kaya and her kids view Tony's kids as entitled and spoiled. Tony's kids see Kaya as mean and bitter. The most defeating conflict, though, is in the marriage. Tony's lack of boundaries with his kids leads Kaya to question her respect for him.

"How can I trust him with our finances when he's a pushover? He can't say no to them, but I can say no to him."

Let's apply the principles of finding unity, overcoming the inertia of past boundaries, and renegotiating boundaries with adult children to Kaya and Tony's circumstances.

In order to find unity, each partner is going to have to do some things. Kaya needs to find patience with her husband. If she

112

doesn't, her frustration will make it harder for him to find the resolve he needs to honor his marriage and change his boundaries with his children. Tony, on the other hand, needs to realize how his paralyzed parenting (his inability to set boundaries) has paralyzed his children, leaving them unable to find direction for their lives or take responsibility for themselves.

When a parent is overly responsible for a child, whether that child is five or thirty-five, they will be under-responsible. When one person is overfunctioning, the other will underfunction. In order to help children become adults, then, a parent's primary job is to become unnecessary. If Tony can accept this truth, then he can find the courage to change how he responds to his children. If he cannot find the courage to change, his children will not mature, and their entitlement will likely lead to the destruction of his own marriage.

So, what might change look like for Tony and Kaya if they overcome the inertia of their current boundaries? With adult children, talking is the first step. But talk is cheap if it doesn't have any action along with it.

Tony might start by owning his past parenting choices and foreshadowing coming changes. Speaking to his three adult children, he might say, "I've come to understand that with my style of parenting I have inadvertently left you guys financially dependent on me. I regret that. Plus, my marriage has brought me some new obligations that I need to consider. So I need us to talk through how you can become more independent." This will start what might be a long and perhaps stressful series of discussions with Tony's kids about change, growing up, and taking responsibility. In our experience, when a permissive parent begins altering life-long boundaries with their children, at least one child is likely to get angry. Becoming responsible is not typically the first choice of people who have never had to be responsible. From their standpoint, this is another unwanted change in their family. And really, who wouldn't want someone else financing their life?

Tony's resolve to see it through will foster new boundaries and new opportunities for his whole family. Kaya's challenge will be to demonstrate patience and partner with Tony in working toward change. Change will happen, even if a child is dragging their feet, through calm persistence. Change is going to happen. Resolve motivates the unmotivated. Coupled with love and understanding, resolve is compelling.

"I get it," Tony might say to an angry child. "You don't want to move out. But this is going to happen. I'm giving you three months to save enough to do it, so it's time to start looking for somewhere to live. You know I love you. That's why this is important. How can I help you take the next step?"

Did you notice that last question? It's a question that makes a statement. Parenting adult boomerang children is a delicate balance in clearly defining your boundaries—what you will share, do, and give with your resources, time, and energy—and not defining theirs. Tony may agree to share his home for an additional three months, and he'll help them prepare to move out, but he won't take responsibility for finding them a place. But no matter what, moving out *is* going to happen.

Emotionally none of this is easy. Boundary issues with boomerang children have above-the-surface and below-the-surface considerations like any other money-merging matter in your home. If you find yourselves stumbling on above-the-surface issues, be sure to look below the surface in order to see what is getting in the way.

The Sandwich Generation

Have you heard of "the sandwich generation"? The vast majority of adults will experience a season of life when they are sandwiched between raising children and caring for aging parents. For a time, both will need care to varying degrees, and both may require financial assistance at varying levels. The emotional, psychological, relational, and financial boundaries around this season of life are numerous, even before we add the complications of a blended family.

114

When Michael and Jessa married and started blending their children and households, Michael's parents were both deceased. Jessa's mother was retired and in good health, living independently and driving her own car. She had a group of friends and activities and did not need much day-to-day assistance from them. That changed one day when Michael and Jessa were on a weekend trip to a bed-and-breakfast. They got a call that Jessa's mother had suffered a stroke. They immediately drove to the hospital.

When a call like that comes, it changes everything. Some seniors have gradually declining health or memory, while others have sudden changes due to something like a stroke or fall. Both have their challenges. A sudden change leaves little time to prepare, while gradual changes can pit adult children and their aging parents against one another when they disagree on the seriousness of parents' declining health or memory. There's nothing easy about having to address a parent's unsafe living situation by making a parent move out of their home or taking away their car keys.

Michael and Jessa realized that weekend that Jessa's mom would never again be able to live at home independently as she did before. All at once, there were four main issues to be addressed:

1. *Who?* Who would provide for her mom's daily care and assistance? A family member or hired caregivers?

2. *Where?* Where would Jessa's mom get the assistance she needed? Her home, their home, or an assisted living facility?

3. *When?* When would Jessa's mom need assistance? With the stroke, she definitely required medical and practical assistance right away, but with physical therapy she might improve to the point where other options would become available. On the other hand, if her health declined, other transitions would be needed. Aging goes through stages, with further declining health leading to more care needs, or improving health allowing people to gain more independence. The question of *when* is a moving target that

must be addressed multiple times, sometimes week-to-week or month-to-month.

4. *How to pay for it?* Dealing with the first three questions is stressful enough for families, but the question of how to pay for care can be overwhelming. Consulting an experienced elder law attorney will greatly reduce the family's stress and provide clear guidance on benefits options, which we will discuss further in chapter 10. Hopefully Jessa has talked to her mother already about her financial plan and assets to help with increased healthcare needs, but all too often, this is not the case.

After leaving the hospital, Jessa's mother went to a rehab facility where she received physical therapy. Meanwhile, Jessa looked at a very nice assisted living facility not far from where she lived, and she and Michael considered moving her into their home. Michael was willing to do this if Jessa thought it would be best, but Jessa struggled with the decision. She felt guilty about what it would do to her marriage to move her mother into their home, especially since Jessa was still working up to fifty hours a week. She knew she wouldn't be available to her mother like she wanted to be.

On top of that, Jessa's oldest daughter was pregnant with their first grandchild. Caring for her mom would impact how much time Jessa could spend babysitting her new granddaughter. There was a lot to consider.

Navigating the Boundaries

The boundary principles shared in the first half of this chapter apply to Michael and Jessa's situation just as much as to parents dealing with adult children. Making decisions together as a couple and protecting your marital unity is just as vital. Getting that right will allow you to utilize these additional principles.

Honoring Our Parents

One way that adult children can honor their aging parents is by ensuring they are cared for as they grow frail and move toward death. Ensuring this care is not an option; negotiating how it will be provided is.

Old age reminds us that death is inevitable and we can't control everything in life. As we age, we all gradually lose strength and control physically, emotionally, and mentally. In caring for an aging parent, we are also reminded that the freedom of the empty nest is limited. There are many things in life that are out of our control.

Not having control is hard. There are seasons in life when you grow comfortable with the idea of being in charge, but the issues of adult children and aging parents bring such illusions to a screeching halt. We're all affected by this reality. Each of us has a vested interest in how it is managed. That's why when it comes to helping our parents age with grace and dignity, each person should have a say in the boundaries of care and provision.

Negotiating Care

As we will explain in chapters 9 and 10 on retirement and healthcare, conversations about the future shouldn't be put off. If your parents are willing, long before it is needed work with your siblings to begin the conversation about your parents' wishes for care. We never know when life circumstances, such as a sudden illness, will surprise us and leave us with more questions than answers.

Ask your parents to share their ideal scenarios for retirement, residence, and healthcare as well as their independence. Separately, initiate a conversation with your siblings, if you have them, about what financial and time availability each of you can offer to help provide care over time. In our experience, there may be many such conversations over time as your parents age and their physical and cognitive abilities decline. Changing circumstances will limit the options available and affect the decisions that you make.

Ultimately, the type of care you can offer to aging parents will come down to your financial resources as much as your good intentions. You might live comfortably on a solid income, but if you have two kids in college when you need to put your parents in a nursing home, you will quickly find yourself financially strapped. In chapter 10, we will discuss how to plan for healthcare and disability. These steps are just as applicable for your parents as for you. But if they have not planned ahead, our best advice for sorting out your options is to talk to an experienced elder law attorney.

What matters most is a commitment to honor your parents in any way you can and a proactive willingness to talk with all parties involved to make mutually agreeable decisions.

Stepsibling Responsibility

Working with adult siblings can be challenging, and bringing in adult stepsiblings to provide care for aging parents can be even more sticky, especially when relationship closeness and loyalty vary. Every family is different, and your family history and relationship dynamics will affect how you and your siblings and stepsiblings approach the discussion.

Multiple studies show that American adults' willingness to care for an aging family member differs depending on whether the person is a biological parent or stepparent. Even though having stepfamily members increases the size of a family by nearly 40 percent, those added family members are connected by weaker bonds, and they don't all have the same sense of responsibility when it comes to sharing the financial and time demands of caregiving.

Adult stepchildren are less likely (but only slightly less so) to make themselves available to or financially responsible for a stepparent. Compared to those caring for their biological married parents, an adult stepchild is 3.69 percent less likely to give money (including loans and gifts over $100) to a parent and stepparent. But they are 13.3 percent less likely to give time (running errands, giving rides, doing chores, and providing hands-on care) to their parent and stepparent.[3]

The implications of this are twofold. First, if you are a stepparent making plans for your own retirement and healthcare, consider that your stepchildren may not provide for you to the same degree they would a biological parent. And second, if you are the adult child of a parent with stepchildren, don't assume that your stepsiblings will match your level of investment in their care.

Communicating honestly with your entire family about your hopes and boundaries around caregiving will help merge expectations and prevent hurt feelings later. It's also important to consider your specific situation, both as a parent and a child. Longer, more established relationships will lead to more care likely to be shared.

Making Health Decisions

If something happened to your aging parent today, would you know who is empowered to make their important healthcare decisions? Are you and your siblings ready and empowered to step in if your aging parent should become too incapacitated to make their own decisions?

In chapter 10, we will discuss the importance of legal documents such as a healthcare power of attorney. Without this legal authority in place before something happens, you might be forced to go through a costly court process to get the judge to appoint a guardian. So if there's just one thing that you can do now to prepare for difficult decisions later, it's this: Make sure your parents have valid power of attorney documents. Be pushy if you have to! Offer to pay for it. It will be worth it if you need to take action on their behalf later.

Self-Care

Honoring your parents should not result in you depleting your bank account or yourself.

Most caregivers know that they shouldn't give *all* their money to the care of an aging relative, but all too often these same people will refuse to ask for emotional or logistical help from family members, their church family, or the community of nonprofit organizations that exists to support senior care. They'll completely deplete their personal energy and well-being.

However, you can't care for your parent (or marriage, or children, or career, etc.) if you don't care for yourself. Balanced, appropriate self-care is not selfish.

Ongoing boundary discussions should include consideration of caregiving breaks for those providing hands-on care. Who will provide substitute care when—and how often—are questions to explore depending on your specific family situation. Giving one another permission—and *yourself* permission—to take a break is critical.

Clearing the Ledger

Some people are good at keeping a ledger of how family members have hurt them and what they feel is owed because of those past transgressions. This emotional ledger plagues relationships with strain, withdrawal, estrangement, and conflict that can last for years. We wish things were different in a relationship, but we stubbornly wait for the other person to take the first step, or we tell ourselves it's not worth another attempt at reconciliation.

But as we and our parents age and health fails, the looming reality of death should make us look once again at the ledger to decide if we will carry the balance into eternity. Is our pride holding us back from clearing the ledger?

If you are carrying a balance on someone else, or if you feel they are carrying one on you, we strongly encourage you to seek forgiveness and reconciliation. Clear the ledger.

PART THREE

Planning for the Future

Long-range planning is a critical part of financing togetherness, provision, and care. In this section we'll help you look far down the road so you can plan for the future.

8

Planning Your Child's Education

Shawn's son Levi is fifteen. Until recently, he lived with his mother, Shawn's former wife, but last summer he moved in with Shawn and Carrie. The high school in their district has a strong science department and a robotics club, and Levi has a gift for math and science. He has started to talk about going to a school like MIT to be an engineer like his dad.

Shawn is supportive but nervous. He knows that paying for college isn't as easy as it was when he went to school. Back then, he could cover half his state university tuition by working two jobs every summer. His parents paid the other half, and Shawn finished his undergraduate degree without any debt.

Now, things are different. Including room and board, the average in-state public school now costs $21,370, and a four-year private school bill is a mind-blowing $48,510 per year, according to the College Board.[1] There is an increased trend to reach beyond the bachelor's for a graduate degree. In the 2016–2017 academic year, the average student spent $24,812 on grad school, according to national education lender Sallie Mae.[2]

123

Even if Levi could find a summer job, it would barely put a dent in that kind of expense, and every year the numbers rise even further out of reach. Shawn doesn't know how much he can contribute to his son's education either. On paper he has a good salary, but he and Carrie have two kids in elementary school, a second mortgage, and no savings. Levi's mom recently divorced again and is having her own financial troubles.

Shawn wants to encourage Levi to pursue his dreams and get a college education, but he doesn't want to give him false hopes. The only way Levi can go to MIT is if the university or the government foots most of the bill.

Sound familiar?

As parents, we want to give our children the best possible future, which today we generally assume includes a college education. Sixty-five percent of jobs in the United States will require a post–high school credential by 2020, according to the Georgetown University Center on Education and the Workforce.[3] And multiple studies show that college graduates earn significantly more over a lifetime than the average person who only completes high school.[4]

But with the skyrocketing costs of higher education, this well-intentioned goal can become an enormous challenge, especially for blended families who already feel their finances stretched thin. Navigating it will require wisdom, organization, and a willingness to communicate.

Talk to Your Child

Before you start worrying about how to pay for that top-notch medical school, stop and listen to your child. By early high school, they're beginning to develop their own dreams, goals, aspirations, and fears about their future, and their ideas may be different than yours.

Paying for an education your child doesn't want or value isn't a smart investment for either of you.

That's what Randall learned. His oldest daughter, Leah, was an above-average high school student, with good grades and involved in lots of activities, especially in the arts. Her passion was custom jewelry design.

For her whole life, Randall had dreamed about her going to his alma mater, the University of Michigan. He'd bought her first U-M Wolverine T-shirt when she was still a baby, and he started planning her first campus visit while she was still a freshman.

Leah rolled her eyes a little at her dad's enthusiasm, but in her senior year she applied to his alma mater and, when she was accepted, enrolled as an art major. From the first month, even Randall could see that it wasn't a good fit. Leah struggled to motivate herself in the classroom and make meaningful social connections. After a difficult first year, she sat down with her parents and explained that she didn't want to stay in Michigan. She wanted to pursue a career in gemology, and she didn't need a liberal arts degree for that. It would be a waste of their money and her time for her to get an education she didn't want or need.

Randall swallowed his disappointment that his daughter wasn't a Wolverine and acknowledged that it had always been his dream, not hers. With his reluctant agreement, Leah left the university and enrolled in a specialized, well-respected professional training program for her area of interest. She thrived there. Within a year, and for less than half the cost of a degree from a four-year school, Leah had a certificate of expertise and a paid apprenticeship as a gemologist. When her peers were just getting their diplomas and setting out, she was already established in a career she loved.

Randall's story is not uncommon. It's natural for parents to want to guide children and to think we see what's best for them. But as they get older, God starts to reveal his own unique plans and callings for them.

One way to help your child identify their calling is to engage them in conversations about their future early and then let them drive, or at least participate in, the decisions related to their future. Talk to them about the classes, activities, or hobbies where they excel. Is there something that they can see in their future? Are there elective classes they can take to capitalize on their strengths?

Help them identify influential adults in your church or community whom your child can talk to or shadow in order to see the realities of different career paths and choices. Are there people who would be willing to write letters of recommendation when the time comes?

Are there schools or programs that your child is excited about? Can they articulate why? Encourage them to take an active role in researching schools, majors, scholarships, and other aspects of their post–high school life.

It's never too early to work with them to prepare for necessary standardized tests. Support them and help them to do their best, but don't despair if they don't do as well as you hoped. As much as possible, restrain from doing too much for them. The more ownership they take in their choices for their future, the more likely their choices will take root and blossom.

Create a College Covenant

When it comes to your child's future after high school, there are a lot of decisions that will need to be made, and those decisions are often time sensitive, expensive, and important. In divorced and blended families, this can lead to conflicts based on a lack of communication or conflicting priorities.

Your child will benefit from knowing that their whole family—which ideally includes both biological parents and any stepparents—is ready to support them. They don't need to hear a parent complaining that "I didn't agree to that" or "I don't think that this is important" when the clock is ticking and the tuition payment is due.

One of the best ways to create this cohesiveness, for your child's sake, is to organize a conversation when your child starts high school with your child, their other parent, and their stepparents, and then at regular intervals after that. Your goal will be to create a College Covenant, in which you all clearly state and agree on your various commitments regarding your child's higher education.

For some parents, this will be difficult, and it may even seem impossible. But for the good of your child, everyone should address these questions.

What resources can each parent commit to their child's education? This may be a difficult question to answer, especially before you know the details of where your child will go to school or how much it will cost. But it helps to be clear and honest with the family about your expectations. Is there a Togetherness Agreement or divorce agreement that spells out parental responsibility to pay for college? Are there college savings or other bank accounts specifically set aside for this purpose? Are there other sources of expected support, like grandparents or savings bonds? What involvement, if any, will your child's stepparents have in contributing to their education?

This is also a good time to clearly lay out what everyone is willing and able to contribute. Are there annual or total spending caps on how much a parent is willing or able to pay?

What resources do you expect your child to contribute to their education? According to Sallie Mae, "Through a combination of income, savings, and borrowing, students covered 30 percent of [college] costs in 2016–2017."[5]

Do you expect your child to get an after-school or summer job when they're old enough and to save their income? Do you expect them to work while they're in college? If loans are taken, is your child solely responsible for repaying them?

Are there limits on the type of education, location, or activity that either parent will support? Your College Covenant agreement is about more than just money. It's about laying out any conditions that come with the financial support. If your child wants to go to school on the other side of the country—or the other side of the world—does that change things? What if they want to go to a more expensive private college instead of an in-state university?

If they want to go to a nontraditional or unaccredited program? A professional trade school? Does your financial commitment include graduate school?

Is there an age or stage (like marriage or parenting) when you would no longer consider yourself responsible for helping to pay for your child's education? Are there expenses (like car repairs and gas, entertainment, computers, phone, travel, etc.) that you don't consider part of higher education?

Is your financial support tied to any requirements for your child, such as maintaining certain grades, moral standards, or freedom from addictions?

Of course, you can't plan ahead for every eventuality, and some of your decisions may change over time. But clarifying your values up front is generally easier than having to face a last-minute decision, when emotions may be high.

Is there a time limit to your financial commitment? Will your College Covenant cover only four years of higher education? According to a 2014 study by Complete College America, only 19 percent of students at the average four-year university actually graduate on time.[6] This happens for a variety of reasons, including credits that are lost when a student changes their major or transfers, the need for many students to work full-time while also attending school, and a general lack of education plans when they first begin.

In order to graduate in four years, students must average about fifteen credit hours per semester. This means taking the courses that match a selected major, not changing that major, and considering summer school if they fall behind.

While every situation is different and your family may have to adjust expectations if the need arises, it's important to set an expectation with your child. Those extra years could add a lot of extra expense for everyone in the family.

How will education funds be collected, and who will oversee them? This is an especially important question for blended families to address. Is your child responsible enough to single-handedly manage funds coming from different places and make appropriate payments on time? Most teenagers right out of high school would struggle with this, and they benefit from some oversight and accountability. For some blended families, though, it may be difficult for one set of parents to send their education payments to the second set of parents.

Discuss in advance the oversight plan that will work for your family. Will each parent send their tuition payments directly to the school? What about other expenses? How can you involve your child in the process to encourage their financial accountability? Can you open an education-specific bank account with your child and their other parent as joint owners? What kind of oversight will the non-custodial parent have regarding the way funds are spent?

Save for College

The sooner you start to discuss your child's future and find common ground as a family, the sooner you can start setting aside funds to cover the costs. It's never too early to create a specific investment or savings plan for your children's future education.

The options can seem complicated and even overwhelming, but it's worth taking the time to understand the various benefits and limitations. Here's a quick summary of seven of the most popular education funding vehicles. To understand how these options fit your family's unique situation, consult with your personal financial advisor.

529 or College Savings Plans: Since 1996, states have provided a specific, self-directed way to save for college through accounts called 529s, which can be applied to the cost of any accredited educational institution, and to some extent K–12 tuition expenses for public, private, and religious schools. 529 plans vary from state to state but are primarily mutual fund investments, though some plans allow separately managed accounts, equity indexed investments, bank CDs, and guaranteed investment contracts. These are often provided in preestablished investment portfolios that offer some flexibility for changes and typically charge annual maintenance, administration, and/or investment fees.

All withdrawals that are spent on qualified educational expenses are federal income tax-free, regardless of your income or age, and some states also provide deductions and tax credits specifically for 529s. Though 529 plan contributions are not federal income tax deductible, the earnings grow federal tax–free and will not be taxed when money is distributed for qualifying educational expenses. Approved education expenses include tuition for full- or part-time enrollment at an accredited college or university, as well as room and board if the student attends at least half-time. If a student does not live on campus and the rent paid to their landlord is greater than the school's room and board costs, then the excess is not a qualified educational expense. Technology such as computers, printers, laptops, internet service, and software required by the school are also valid expenses, as are books and supplies. If the money is used for any other purpose, it is taxed and penalized.

A 529 account is established in one person's name, typically the parent's, so you, not your child, will manage decisions about the account. This also means that the 529 is considered your asset rather than your child's, a beneficial distinction on the FAFSA that we'll discuss later in the chapter. There are annual and total contribution limits, which vary based on the cost of higher education in that state. However, anyone can contribute to a 529 account, including your child or other family members.[7]

Currently, more than thirty states offer a tax deduction or credit for contributions into their state-sponsored 529 plans. Deduction amounts vary by state, ranging from about $500 per year to the full amount of the contribution. Most states that offer this deduction or credit require you to use your home state's plan to qualify for the tax benefit, but Arizona, Kansas, Minnesota, Missouri, Montana, and Pennsylvania residents are eligible for tax breaks when contributing to any other state's plan.

Prepaid College Tuition Plans: Parents pay money to a fund managed either by their state or a private university, essentially buying college credits at slightly above current market prices. They can then cash those credits in to pay for tuition, and with some plans also room and board, when their child heads off to school years in the future. Some plans even let parents use excess tuition credits for other qualified expenses.

Prepaid college tuition plans typically charge enrollment and annual investment fees. They offer the same tax benefits as self-directed 529s but offer the security of being detached from the fluctuations of the market if there is a recession.

The bigger risk for a prepaid plan, of course, is that you can only spend it on an in-state public college or at the private college where the account is established. If your child determines that they will seek their education elsewhere, only the principal will be refunded to you.

This type of investment is not available in every state, and only a handful of private colleges offer programs like this. For an up-to-date list, visit SavingForCollege.com/compare_529_plans/.

Mutual Funds: Some families set aside their education funds in an investment account that is not specifically designated for education. This gives them more flexibility in how they use the funds in the future. A mutual fund account gives you a wide range of nearly unlimited investment choices. While you don't receive the same tax benefits as an education-labeled plan—taxes must be paid annually on any dividends, interest, or realized capital gains—you also won't be penalized for withdrawing funds for non-education reasons.

Roth IRA: Another popular investment and savings opportunity is a Roth IRA. Because this is officially a retirement account, money saved here is not counted by the government when it assesses your financial aid package (discussed later in the chapter). Because of this, some families include a Roth IRA as part of their College Covenant. They agree that the student will take out loans to pay for college. In some cases, the interest from those loans will be tax deductible while the student is in school. The student's

131

parents, meanwhile, make annual contributions to a Roth IRA. If the student maintains their end of the family's covenant—e.g., maintaining certain grades, graduating on time, staying out of trouble, etc.—the parents will take a single, tax-free distribution from their Roth accounts to pay off (or down, depending on their financial situation) the loan amount.

There are some income limitations on Roths, but most middle-class American individuals can contribute up to $6,000 per year to a Roth IRA, or $7,000 if they're over fifty (2019 limits). The funds grow tax-free, and the principal can be withdrawn tax-free for qualified reasons, including education expenses. Earnings on the account are also tax-free if you are over fifty-nine and a half and have had your account for at least five years.

Usually about here someone asks about traditional IRAs. If a family is strapped paying for college, should they consider tapping in to their traditional IRA account? The answer is almost never. Or only as a last resort.

Between them Suzanne and Joe had four kids, ages fifteen to twenty-four. Her oldest had just graduated from college before they married, but Peter, her youngest, would be a college freshman in the fall, and Joe's two high school students would be following close behind.

After filling out the FAFSA, the Free Application for Federal Student Aid, and applying for Peter's financial aid, the couple got a bit of sticker shock. Their expected family contribution was much higher than it had been for Suzanne's oldest. When he went to college, Suzanne was single and her household income more limited. As a result he received a lot of financial aid and loans, and the immediate family contribution was low.

With Peter it was a different story. Now that Suzanne and Joe had married, Joe's income was also considered in determining financial aid options. The increased household income translated into a much bigger family contribution.

They explored tapping in to their traditional IRAs to help pay for college. Suzanne had a nice-sized IRA that she received when she divorced, and Joe had an IRA he had rolled over from the 401(k) at his former job. They decided to ask their estate planning attorney if it was a good idea.

"Usually an IRA should only be used for college funding as an absolute last resort," he said. "There are some big pitfalls; let me walk you through it. It is called an 'individual retirement account' because the government intends it for retirement. If you take out money before age fifty-nine and a half, there is a 10 percent penalty."[8]

"Yikes. That does not sound good," said Suzanne.

"And that's not all," their attorney continued. "IRAs, other than Roth IRAs, have never been taxed. For instance, Joe's old 401(k) that is now in an IRA was not taxed when you put money in, but it will be when you take money out. So if you take money out for college, you'll have to take money out for taxes—in addition to the 10 percent penalty.

"I ran the numbers so you can see my point. Let's assume you're in a 22 percent tax bracket and you need $25,000 for college. Taking out that IRA money bumps you up to a 24 percent tax bracket. Guess how much you would have to take out of the IRA to end up with $25,000? Almost $38,000!" he said. "It would cost you about $13,000 in penalties and taxes, and you'd only get to use about two-thirds of your IRA money for their college bill."

Using traditional IRA money is one of the most expensive ways to get college funds. Not only are there taxes and a penalty, but you also lose out on any future investment growth for retirement.

Savings Bonds, Series EE or Series I: One of the most secure options, though perhaps returning the lowest yield on investment, is to purchase traditional savings bonds. These are easy to purchase—with a minimum investment of just $25 if you buy online—and are backed by the full faith and credit of the US government. Bonds start earning interest the month after you purchase them and continue to earn interest for twenty or thirty years, depending on the type. However, they can be cashed in without penalties after just five years.

A benefit of savings bonds is that if you use the cashed-in bond to pay for certain educational expenses, like tuition, the income is exempt from federal income tax, within certain income limitations.

UGMA (Uniform Gift to Minors Act) and UTMA (Uniform Transfer to Minors Act): Under special categories, a person (like a noncustodial parent or a grandparent) can gift money or securities to a minor through a custodial account, typically administered by the custodial parent until the child is eighteen or twenty-one, depending on the state. These are invested in the child's name and Social Security number and can include nearly unlimited investment choices.

These UGMA and UTMA accounts are custodial accounts using the minor's Social Security number. Therefore, because the accounts are technically owned by the student, they must be reported as investments on the FAFSA under the asset category of the student. This is the case even if the titling looks something like "[Parent or grandparent's name] as custodian for [child's name] under the [child's state of residence] Uniform Gift to Minors or Uniform Transfer to Minor's Act." Later on in this chapter we will discuss how different types of income and assets are evaluated.

The accounts are subject to normal fees and administration charges, and earnings are not tax deferred. Funds can be withdrawn by the custodian for educational or other specific needs of the child.

Coverdell Education Savings Accounts: This investment option is also sometimes referred to as an ESA. It is similar to a 529 in its tax benefits, as long as proceeds are spent on approved educational expenses at qualified institutions. Parents can contribute up to $2,000 a year for every child in their household under eighteen. Additional contributions are subject to an excise tax. Unlike with a Roth IRA, contributions are not subject to proof of the contributor's earned income, so a child could contribute to their own ESA. Like other tax-protected savings plans, there are income restrictions, and the account is subject to administration fees.

An ESA account must be used for the sole benefit of the child, and distributions are paid to the student beneficiary, not the parent. However, the account is considered a parental asset for FAFSA filing, which may result in additional financial aid, since a parental asset is counted less than a student's asset.

Until 2018, the Coverdell ESA was the only vehicle that included funding for private elementary and high school expenses. Since 2018, though, the 529 has been expanded to also fund precollege education.

Understand Options for Financial Aid

The sticker shock of college pricing comes with some relief. According to the College Board, over 70 percent of full-time students received grants in 2011–2012 to help lighten the load.[9]

While only 0.2 percent of students receive $25,000 or more in scholarships,[10] almost one-third of all college costs nationwide are covered by grants and scholarships, which don't need to be repaid.[11] Scholarships and grants come from a variety of sources. Many are offered directly through the college or university, but some private, nonprofit, state, church, and community organizations also offer funding. High school guidance counselors are often good sources of information about available scholarships in the area.

Education funds that can't be paid through family or student savings, or a grant or scholarship, are generally covered by some form of education loan. More than 70 percent of all students now borrow money to help pay for college. Each year we hear that the newest class of graduates carries even more debt than any students before them[12], and college graduates today report that their debt makes it harder to buy a home or live independently. According to college planning website Edvisors, a study found that due to the sometimes overwhelming debt loads students are taking on, the normal life events of marriage and purchasing a home are being delayed.[13]

Lumping all "borrowing" into one category can be deceiving, though, because there are a variety of ways for families to acquire the funds to pay for college, and some are more advantageous than others.

Here's a short summary of the most common types of loans.

Subsidized Stafford Loans

These are provided by the federal government for students with above-average financial need. The government pays the loan interest that accrues while the student is in school and offers flexible repayment plans that include a grace period after graduation and the option for deferment.

Unsubsidized Stafford Loans

These are also provided directly to students by the federal government but without the strict need-based formula. The government does not pay the interest on these loans, which will accrue with the balance while the student is in school.

PLUS (Parent Loan for Undergraduate Students)

These federally issued loans come with low, fixed interest rates and are offered to parents of undergraduate or graduate students.

Perkins Loans

These are limited, federally issued loans for undergraduate and graduate students with exceptional financial need. They are only available at certain schools.

Private Education Loans

These are offered by a variety of private lenders to supplement federally guaranteed loans. They come with a variety of interest rates, repayment obligations, and requirements that are generally less favorable than federally insured and supported loans.

The specific formulas for financial aid, including interest rates, estimated family contributions, maximum annual allowances, and total available funds, change often. For up-to-date information, worksheets, calculators, and news, here are three valuable websites:

- StudentAid.ed.gov—the US Department of Education's financial aid resource
- FinAid.org
- SavingForCollege.com

Get Organized Early

In order to take advantage of the various financial aid options available to you and your child, you'll need to be organized and have access to a variety of information. As your child progresses through high school, encourage them to make a calendar of deadlines and activities that will help them pursue their college plans, along with key names and contact information for follow-up. The closer they get to graduation, the more deadlines will come up, so starting early will help them build responsibility.

Here's a calendar of action steps you can take each year.

Freshman Year

If possible, sit down as a family—with your child's other parent—and agree on a College Covenant. This plan may change over time as your financial and family situations change, but it's important to get everyone on the same page early.

Encourage your child to take the most challenging courses they can manage and to try a variety of school and community activities. Are there opportunities for volunteer or leadership roles?

Freshman year is also the best time to create a filing system where you can collect and easily access documents in the following categories:

- **Academics and activities.** Help your child save high school report cards, transcripts, test scores, letters of recognition and recommendation, awards, and records of community, church, and volunteer service.
- **Family background.** Collect as much information as you can about your child's family, including grandparents and great-grandparents. Include each person's work and educational background, ethnicity and country of origin, religious background and affiliations, and past experiences. Many private scholarships are established to honor unique talents or histories.
- **Financial information.** Be sure to save your tax records, W-2s, paycheck stubs, child support payment records (made or received), bank and brokerage account statements, and retirement plan statements.
- **Scholarship research.** Don't wait until the last minute to start researching scholarships and grants. Create a file where you and your child can collect information about both merit-based and need-based programs for which they may be eligible.
- **Completed applications.** Once you start filling out forms, you'll realize that you're often called on to answer the same questions over and over. Keep copies of your completed applications to save time and track your responses.

Sophomore Year

In the fall, look at your own finances and consider any possible restructuring opportunities that would minimize your Expected Family Contribution, which we'll explore more in the following sections. The FAFSA will look at your income and financial statements for the year *previous* to the year you file, and two years before your child actually begins college, so your finances now will affect your child's financial aid package in three years.

Encourage your child to start thinking about their future. Ask them to make a college wish list of where they think they'd like to go and what they'd like to study. It's not too soon to start researching these schools' scholarship and other financial aid opportunities. If your child is an athlete, this is the year that college athletic recruiters will start paying attention.

Your child's school may also recommend or administer a practice SAT or ACT. If you are serious about maximizing your student's scores, consider taking prep classes from experts.

Junior Year

Colleges and universities will review junior year grades and activities carefully when they consider high school senior applicants. Encourage your child to be focused and diligent about their studies and to take on leadership opportunities in their school, church, or community. If they can handle Advanced Placement classes, this is the year to take them.

Help your student prepare for the SAT or ACT in the spring and again consider taking prep classes. The SAT score is half math and half a combination of reading and English. The ACT score is more balanced with science, math, English, and reading each being about one-fourth. According to Jason Franklin of Better Prep Success, Inc., because the ACT test includes science, and the SAT does not, more college-bound students are taking the ACT.[14] Nationally, more scholarship opportunities come from the ACT because of this science component and the more balanced scoring. Franklin also suggests taking the ACT more than once, as only your highest test scores are used.[15] Consider having your junior student take the ACT in December. It allows you to buy back a copy of the test and your student's answers, called Test Information Release (TIR). This information can then be used, with an ACT prep class, to work on the areas needing improvement for the April and/or June test dates. ACT tests are given in April, June, July (in most states), September, October, December, and February, but only the December, April, and June tests offer Test Information Release (see ACTStudent.org).

Now is also the time for your student to ask teachers, leaders, supervisors, and other adults who know them well for letters of recommendation. Your junior should also start working on their college application essays. These essays, even if 250 words or less, have a very significant impact on college scholarship offers. Consider having an English teacher or professional editor help them with their essays.

Start attending college fairs and visiting a few of your child's top school choices. Talk with them about what they see, and help them imagine the costs and benefits of their options. Include your child's other parent in this as much as possible, given your unique situation.

Senior Year

The fall months are the time that all of your earlier organization will pay off. As soon as possible, help your child fill out and submit applications to the schools and programs that they choose and that are consistent with the family's College Covenant. This would be a good time to gather everyone together again to reaffirm each person's commitments and priorities.

The FAFSA and most state financial aid forms for the following academic year are available October 1 and should be submitted as soon as possible after that, since many schools and states distribute money on a first-come-first-serve basis. You will submit information based on the *previous calendar year to the year that you're filing*, using the information filed with the previous year's taxes.

The FAFSA

The Free Application for Federal Student Aid, or FAFSA, is the core document that determines your child's chance of receiving financial aid. This standardized form determines what a student is eligible to receive, and from there, individual colleges will provide their offers.

The primary outcome of the FAFSA is what's called your Expected Family Contribution, or EFC. This spells out exactly how much the government thinks that your child's family should be able to contribute toward their education. All of the decisions about federal funds, and many state and even private need-based scholarships, are dependent on your EFC.

The FAFSA is deceptively short for its importance, taking the average student just twenty-three minutes to complete, yet there are several important things to note and consider in advance that could make significant impacts on the outcome. The most important question for the child of a blended family, who may shuttle between two households with distinct financial situations, is the question of which parent's income should be reported on the form.

The answer may surprise you, because the FAFSA is controlled and regulated by the US Department of Education, and they have different rules and standards about defining dependents than other government organizations, like the IRS.

If parents of a student submitting a FAFSA are legally divorced or separated, and they live apart, the "custodial parent" by FAFSA standards is the parent your child *lived with for the most calendar days* of the year previous to the date the FAFSA is submitted, regardless of whether they are the parents with legal custody.

The FAFSA formula takes into account only the custodial parent's income and assets, as well as those of their spouse (your child's stepparent), if applicable, regardless of whether that stepparent has agreed to help fund the child's education. Even if there is a prenuptial agreement in place that says the new spouse is not financially responsible for their stepchild's education, the government will consider their income. Their reasoning is that the government is not bound by a legal agreement (the prenup) between two other parties, and including the stepparent's information on the FAFSA helps create a full and complete picture of the student's family's real finances and reasonable Expected Family Contribution.

At the same time, the FAFSA does not take into account any income or assets of the noncustodial parent, regardless of how involved that parent is in the child's life.

So let's suppose that high school sophomore Brandon's mother and stepfather are both physicians. Together, they make more than $500,000 per year. Brandon's father is unmarried and works as a middle school English teacher, with a total household income of $70,000. Brandon's mother and father have joint custody, and Brandon moves between their homes as his dual residences. The balance is so even that he ends up spending 182 and 183 days in the houses, respectively.

If they plan and work together, Brandon's parents have a tremendous opportunity to work cooperatively for their child's best interest. If Brandon spends 183 days in the year before they file the FAFSA with his doctor mother, then she and her husband are Brandon's custodial parents, and his chance for need-based financial aid is very low. On the other hand, if Brandon spends 183 days with his teacher dad, then he could be eligible for substantial scholarships and grants. The practical difference for both families is small, but the opportunity for Brandon is huge.

Of course, every family situation is different, and many blended families have other, more pressing issues to consider when it comes to custody arrangements and time spent with noncustodial parents. You'll need to make a decision about what's best for your family and then review it in the College Covenant.

The second important thing to consider when planning for the FAFSA is how different types of income and assets are evaluated. When the federal government determines the EFC, they make assumptions about the percentage of money that a family should be able to contribute to their child's education. Those percentages vary according to the type of asset. For example, the FAFSA assumes that as much as 50 percent of a student's income, above a protected amount, should be contributable as well as 22–47 percent of the custodial parents' income. It also takes a percentage of the student's and a much smaller percentage of parents' nonretirement assets, including savings and investments. The FAFSA does not take into account other categories of assets like home equity, small business equity, qualified retirement plans, life insurance cash value, or personal possessions.

Knowing this, your family can make some decisions or reallocations in order to make the best FAFSA case for your child. Again, each situation is different, especially with blended families, and before you do anything you should discuss it with your personal financial advisor.

However, it may help you to know that other families have been able to make a stronger FAFSA case by

- using assets like underperforming CDs or savings accounts to pay down debts,
- building equity in a home or business by spending assets to make material improvements,
- maximizing contributions to 401(k)s, IRAs, and other retirement plans,
- adding value to permanent life insurance policies,
- investing in tax-sheltered annuities (though not counted by FAFSA, they are counted on some other aid forms), and
- making sure savings and investments are owned by parents, not the student.

One final question that comes up often in these discussions is about the assets and contributions of grandparents. If your child's grandparents are interested in contributing to your child's college education, remind them to meet with a financial advisor to determine the best way to handle it. If they give money directly to your child for their tuition, it could be considered income for the student and must be reported on the next year's financial aid forms.

Consider the Alternatives

As you're running the numbers and considering the options, don't forget that higher education planning also means considering alternatives to traditional four-year programs. These can be beneficial to your child if they're not ready to take on the responsibilities of an expensive education.

Local and two-year colleges: Typically called community colleges or junior colleges, these two-year, nonresidential public schools provide an affordable pathway to a traditional four-year degree. More than 40 percent of all undergraduate students in the United States attend community colleges, which charge a fraction of the cost of a major private university. Community colleges also help students who don't have the grades or maturity for the full experience of independent living ease into the college experience. Most community college students continue to live with their families and have flexible schedules that can accommodate employment or other family obligations.

Trade schools, certificates, and associate degrees: As we saw earlier with the example of Randall and his daughter Leah, not every high school graduate needs to get a four-year degree from a liberal arts school. Many young people are drawn to technical or specialized careers, and they can pursue their dreams with certification programs or associate degrees, which cost less time and money while providing hands-on experience.

Military programs: Generations of young Americans have found ways to tie together national service and higher education. A small, select group attend military academies across the country. These are rigorous schools that draw thousands of applicants and demand the very best examples of academic and physical ability and leadership qualities. In exchange, students are given a full scholarship, a guaranteed officer commission in the military after graduation, and an experience they'll carry with them for their whole lives.

For thousands of other high school graduates, the path to their future doesn't start in a classroom. Those who enlist in the

American military after earning a high school diploma and who show aptitude will be given on-the-job training in dozens of career tracks. Later, they can take advantage of the military's generous GI Bill and tuition reimbursement to earn a degree while they're in the service.

Others enlist in ROTC, the Reserve Officers' Training Corps, in which a student attends a traditional four-year college under a full scholarship paid by the specific branch of the military sponsoring the program. They take classes with the general student body and pursue the major of their choice, but they also receive basic military and officer leadership training, and upon graduation with a bachelor's degree, they commit to a certain number of years of either active duty or active reserve duty.

In the end, the education opportunities open to your child are as unique and interesting as your kids are. Being part of a blended family doesn't have to limit their future options. Instead, with the right planning and lots of communication, it can open their world to twice as many possibilities.

Planning Your Retirement

B ob and Tamara met at a conference where Bob was a speaker and Tamara an aspiring social worker from the Dominican Republic. They married with four children ranging from eighteen to thirty-six. As Bob approaches age sixty-five, he and a much younger Tamara (forty-nine) find themselves making some of the biggest money decisions yet in their relationship.

The couple enjoys each other deeply and has many similar interests. But through the years their differing philosophies about money have led to conflict. Now, preparing for Bob's retirement is bringing them great stress. Tamara grew up working in the office at her family's sugarcane operation in the Dominican Republic. She has always been frugal, and she shies away from the stock market. Her father nearly lost the business "gambling with the family savings" in the roaring stock market of the nineties, and again with high-tech stocks in 2001–2003. So Tamara is insisting that Bob wait until age seventy to take Social Security in order to maximize their future income and protect their $273,000 in FDIC-insured certificates of deposit. Bob, on the other hand, is an aggressive stock market investor with over 70 percent of his 401(k) in the global markets, and he wants to retire and take his Social Security right now. Up until now, Bob's $400,000 retirement account has averaged over 9 percent earnings per year since he has known Tamara, but the markets are at an all-time high, interest rates are rising, and many industry experts see an economic recession coming.

What should Bob and Tamara do? What is the answer to their wide differences in personal risk tolerance? When should Bob take his Social Security? How much income will they need, and what are the best investment vehicles for the Russells to both live well and, just as important, to sleep well at night free from worry?

The answers are not simple. According to the Social Security website, a male aged sixty-five today can expect to live nearly another twenty years, and females at the same age another twenty-one years.[1] If you are younger, there may be even longer life ahead in your golden years. Whether you and your spouse decide to retire in the traditional sense of spending time without a paycheck or you will be "re-firing" into a second career or life passion, a financial plan is vital to experiencing your best futures.

Certainly, the old adage "time is money" is true when it comes to planning for retirement. Yet a poll by the Employee Benefit Research Institute shows that only 17 percent of American workers are "very confident" that they will have enough money saved for retirement.[2] According to the Employee Benefit Research Institute, if your goal is to replace about 80 percent of your current income for that fourth quarter of life, with the average American earning just over $50,000 a year, a person in their twenties needs to start saving 9 to 13 percent of their income on a consistent basis and using the advice of a good financial planning team to diversify investments. If you don't start until your forties, that percentage of savings goes up to about 19 percent annually![3] The burden just gets heavier for those who start saving for retirement after forty, so wherever you are, the best time to get started is now.

At the same time, it seems like many middle-aged folks would rather clean their bathrooms than plan for retirement. Bob and Tamara certainly feel that way, and you may agree. Why do you think that is the case? Perhaps it's our dependence upon government programs such as Social Security. (We will talk more about Social Security later in this chapter.) Or maybe some are part of the few remaining workers who still enjoy a defined benefit pension plan. This, plus a 401(k) with company matching contributions, may leave one with no sense of need for additional planning.

More likely, though, a hesitation to talk about retirement planning is because good habits are hard to get started. It may be difficult to face up to the fact that you aren't as prepared for those future decades as you should be. Starting your retirement planning may be hindered by a bad experience with a product salesperson, or there is just no one you know whom you can trust with this enormous project. Plus, the average stepfamily may have additional expenses such as child support and alimony and may not feel that they can do much in the way of retirement planning at this time.

It doesn't need to be so intimidating. Let's look at the steps that are involved in the retirement planning process so that you can see a well-defined path to move forward.

The Five-Step Retirement Planning Process

Step 1. Where Would We Like to Be, and Who Can Help Us Get There?

Before you act, take the time to envision your retirement (or *re-firement*). Create a retirement map together.

Individually and together as a couple, spend time thinking and dreaming. This is the time that will make all the other steps effective. What is important to you? Do you dream of retirement in the traditional sense, kicking back and not working, or do you want the chance to reinvent yourselves in a second career, a life passion, or both?

It's important to be realistic here as well. This is the time to come to grips with any possible retirement obstacles and mitigate or eliminate the threat of unexpected expenses to your investment portfolios. A blended family like Bob and Tamara's or yours may have even more moving parts than a traditional family. Will you need to navigate the sandwich years of having to support children in college and potentially several aging parents? Are you prepared financially for an unexpected illness or disability? How many others in your blended family are depending upon your income for support both now and in the future?

A retirement planning team can help you tackle and address a myriad of questions, scenarios, issues, and risks in this arena. Could you get by with a do-it-yourself retirement plan? Sure, but having a retirement planning team will greatly increase your chances of reaching your financial goals in retirement. Not everyone needs each and every member of the team. Who you get to help and the number of advisors needed depends on the complexity of your finances and the number of issues you want to address. In that way, retirement planning is a lot like cooking up some food in your kitchen. There is a big difference between the preparation and expertise needed to prepare yourself a microwavable snack and to serve a formal gourmet dinner for three families coming over. So do consider having at least one other pair of eyes looking over your shoulder.

We recommend that you talk with family and friends who share your values and life situations. Ask them for referrals to trusted retirement planning professionals, and then interview two or three of them before you make the decision to engage their services.

Here are some good questions to ask those you are considering hiring:

- What types of financial services does this individual provide?
- Are they a professional who can address a broad range of questions, or are they a specialist in one area, such as investment planning or tax planning?

150

- What licenses and registrations do they have?
- How are they compensated? Is there a fee-only system to develop your plan for an agreed-upon amount, plus commission, or are they paid solely on commission? This might have more bearing on what they recommend than you may think.
- Will they include your spouse and children in a family planning project if that's what you want?
- Will they have time to handle your case, or do they seem overworked and harried?
- Do they have an organized office and desk, or does it seem chaotic with papers everywhere?
- Do you get the feeling that they are interested in your case and want to help you succeed?
- Will they handle your case personally or as part of a team? Will you be comfortable if the management of your plan is handed off to others?
- Do they have the credentials (for example, as an attorney to draft documents or CPA to coordinate tax implications) to handle the complexity of your situation? Here is a limited list of the prevalent titles and acronyms used by retirement planning professionals and what they stand for:
  - **CFP:** Certified Financial Planner. These individuals specialize in financial planning, including investments, estate, tax, and retirement planning.
  - **ChFC:** Chartered Financial Consultant. They provide assistance with comprehensive financial and business planning, including the creation and conservation of wealth, retirement planning, and estate, gift, and trust taxation.
  - **CLU:** Chartered Life Underwriter. They have expertise in life, disability, and long-term care insurance, as

151

well as financial, estate, retirement, business, and employee benefit planning, including pensions and group benefits.

- **CPA:** Certified Public Accountant. Their expertise is in tax planning for individuals and businesses.
- **EA:** Enrolled Agent. These are tax experts licensed to represent clients before the IRS.

Step 2. Where Are We Today?

Take an inventory of your current situation. Have you made or updated your lists of assets, determined the time horizons on each goal, identified your individual risk profiles,[4] and discussed as a couple any special situations, such as how you would wish to help a child with special needs or transfer a family business?

This step is often the hardest because it is so meticulous. It's easy to get overwhelmed or to put it off because there are more immediate needs. Don't be discouraged as you begin to assess each and every asset and liability. Many couples have to agree to put this inventory phase on their calendar twice a year in order not to have this crucial but sometimes excruciatingly meticulous area fall way down in priority. Usually one of the two of you is better with record keeping and can be the gatekeeper of the financial books and help keep this process on track.

It is very important to take your time and identify the ownership on every financial asset and liability. Though ownership of assets applies directly to how your estate is eventually going to be distributed, both ownership and beneficiary structure can have an impact on retirement income. For example, who owns an annuity and who is named as the annuitant on that annuity will determine whose life expectancy is used to calculate income amounts and who ultimately has control of that income stream. Often the ownership of an asset will have an impact on the taxation of that asset and then ultimately determine who in the blended family gets what and when.

Also include any planning documents, such as your wills, trusts and trustees, and powers of attorney. (We'll talk more about these in chapters 10 and 11.)

Step 3. How Do We Get There?

Once you know what you have to work with, you can determine your best retirement plan vehicle.

TRADITIONAL IRA

A traditional IRA is an individual retirement account that lets your earnings grow tax-deferred. Anyone younger than seventy and a half with earned income can open and contribute to a traditional IRA.

Depending upon your income and tax filing status, you may qualify for a tax deduction on the money you contribute each year. As with many of the retirement plans that we will discuss, both the amount you can contribute and the amount of the deductibility of your deposits depend upon income ranges that differ according to your tax filing status. Check with your financial advisor team or online information to keep up with these figures that change frequently.

Traditional IRAs allow the account holder to begin taking penalty-free distributions starting at age fifty-nine and a half. Prior to that age there is a 10 percent premature distribution penalty in addition to the ordinary income tax. However, even before age fifty-nine and a half you can withdraw certain amounts from your traditional IRA account without the normal 10 percent premature distribution penalty for qualified first-time home buyer expenses and for qualified higher education expenses. Hardships such as disability and certain levels of unreimbursed medical expenses may also exempt you from penalty, though all of these distributions are still subject to ordinary income taxes. The traditional IRA then requires you to start taking what are called "required minimum distributions" or RMDs, of a certain percentage of your account when you turn seventy and a half.

Roth IRA

The Roth IRA provides no income-tax deduction on contributions, but the earnings and withdrawals of principal are generally tax-free within some guidelines. Like with the traditional IRA, there are annual contribution limits, with an additional $1,000 annual catch-up contribution allowed for those over fifty years of age. There are no age restrictions, but there are income eligibility restrictions. The Roth IRA eligibility restrictions are adjusted gross income phase-out ranges, and as with the traditional IRA these phase outs change each year. See your advisor for current numbers.

If you earn too much, you are not eligible to open a Roth IRA. Yes, unfortunately, people who earn too much to contribute to a Roth IRA are at a disadvantage without this option, which provides tax-free income in retirement. If this is the case, however, there is a potential work-around. You could open a nondeductible IRA and convert it to a Roth IRA. This is called a "backdoor Roth"—you contribute to a traditional IRA without the deduction, due to your higher income phase-out limits, then convert or change this traditional IRA to a Roth IRA. You will need an advisor's help with this strategy as there are key questions you must address prior to using the backdoor Roth. There are no income restrictions for Roth IRA conversions. For those at age seventy and a half, Roth IRAs do not require minimum distributions the way that traditional IRAs do. Not having to take required minimum distributions at age seventy and a half allows you to defer taxes that much longer, thereby increasing your income stream when you do begin taking income for retirement. Whether you should consider the traditional or the Roth IRA is a good topic to bring to your advisor(s).

SEP IRA

If you are self-employed or own a small business, then the SEP IRA may be the right retirement plan vehicle for you. The SEP IRA is available for self-employed individuals and small-business owners. As with each of these retirement planning tools, the amount allowed in SEP IRAs changes frequently and can be found on various websites or with your financial advisor's guidance. SEP IRAs are easy to set up using a two-page form and have low start-up and operating costs. If you are an employer establishing SEP IRAs, you must offer them to all employees who are at least twenty-one years old, have been employed by the employer for three of the last five years, and have had even a few hundred dollars of compensation. These plans usually have a wide range of investment choices, and flexible annual contributions from employers can range from 0–25 percent of compensation. Employers usually must contribute the same percentage of pay for each employee, though they may skip contributions year to year.

SIMPLE IRA

SIMPLE IRAs are also tax-deferred retirement plans designed for small businesses, provided that the business has fewer than one hundred employees. There is simplified IRS reporting in the SIMPLE IRA, which makes it easy to install. There are contribution limits for both the employer and the employee with SIMPLE IRAs. These change frequently and can be found on various websites or with your financial advisor.

If you own a small business and establish SIMPLE IRAs, you must contribute in one of two ways: Either the company must match employee contributions dollar-for-dollar up to 3 percent of the employee's compensation, or it must make a fixed contribution of 2 percent of compensation for all eligible employees even if the employees choose not to contribute. Employer contributions are not subject to Social Security, Medicare, or federal unemployment (FUTA) taxes. The setup and maintenance fees on most SIMPLE IRAs are usually low and may either be paid for by the employer or deducted from employee participants' accounts.

401(K)

The Investment Company Institute estimates that in 2016 about fifty-five million American workers actively participated in 401(k) plans through their employers.[5] The 401(k) plan allows you to defer paying taxes on the amounts you contribute, and often employers offer matching contributions. This has made the 401(k) plan a very popular choice, and if you have one, certainly take advantage of making your pretax salary deferrals at least up to the level of your employer's matching contributions. As with each of these retirement planning tools, the amount allowed for contributions to 401(k)s changes frequently and can be found on various websites or with your financial advisor(s). Most plans allow hardship withdrawals, and some allow penalty-free, in-service withdrawals after age fifty-nine and a half. Like the traditional IRA, the 401(k) has required minimum distributions by age seventy and a half.

SIMPLE 401(K)

Designed for smaller businesses with one to one hundred employees, this plan is a subset of the 401(k) plan. In the SIMPLE format, an employer must make either a matching contribution up to 3 percent of each employee's pay or a nonelective contribution of 2 percent of each eligible employee's pay. Other differences are that SIMPLE 401(k)s are not subject to all the federal retirement plan rules, employees are fully vested in their ownership of all contributions, and there are optional participant loans and hardship withdrawals allowed.

ROTH 401(K)

Unlike with the traditional or SIMPLE 401(k), if you contribute to a Roth 401(k), you contribute from your paycheck after taxes have been withheld. Then at retirement, qualified withdrawals are distributed tax-free.

403(B)

In some blended families, one or both spouses are employees of school systems, nonprofit hospitals, religious organizations, and other tax-exempt 501(c)(3) organizations. The 403(b) may be available for you to plan for retirement. Plan participants make pretax payroll contributions, and some organizations match the employees' deferrals. All full-time employees must be offered participation with some exceptions. As with each of these retirement planning tools, these participation exceptions and the amount allowed for 403(b) contributions change frequently and can be found on various websites or with your financial advisor(s).

Roth 403(b)

The Roth 403(b) plans are based upon the same structure as the 403(b) above, but participants make only post-tax contributions from their paychecks. As with traditional 403(b)s, some organizations match the employee's deferrals.

Step 4. Where do we start?

As challenging as budgeting for most blended families can be, we recommend that you set up the family budget with the intention that you will pay yourself first. You may even have to make yourself a stack of "pay myself" bills and put these reminders where you write checks or keep your household budget records. If you think of your retirement account as the first bill you *must* pay each month, that consistency will help you build wealth over time. But with all of the demands already on your paycheck, how can you even think about setting more money aside? The key is to make it an automated process that you don't even know is happening.

If you have an employer that offers matching contributions in a retirement program, enroll in it and contribute at least the maximum percentage that your employer will match. Sign up for automated salary deferral, where the money is taken out of your paycheck before you ever see it so that you're not tempted to spend it on something else.

If there is no retirement plan program at your place of employment, set up automatic deposits that transfer money monthly from your primary account into an investment account. If money is tight, start with as little as $25 per month.

Think that setting aside such a small amount won't make a difference? Consider this: If you invest $100 per month in an account with a moderate 6 percent annual return on that money, you'll have $8,370 in just six years, over $20,000 in twelve years, and over $37,000 in eighteen years! If you stretch yourself to invest $250 per month, you are looking at almost $21,000 in six years, over $50,000 in twelve years, and a big $92,000 in eighteen years. For those willing and able to pay themselves $500 per month, they'll save over $41,000 by year six, over $101,000 by year twelve, and a whopping $185,000 by the eighteenth year.

Whatever you can add, and however old you are, the time to get started is now.

Step 5. How can we stay on track?

When you're setting off on a thirty-five-year plan for retirement, you'll need to review and realign your process periodically in order to identify and overcome the potential obstacles you're sure to encounter. Set up annual reviews with your retirement planning team, comparing your projections against actual performance.

There are three big enemies to achieving our retirement planning goals: taxes, market volatility, and unforeseen life events.

Though we have no direct control over changing tax laws or our individual tax brackets, we can choose tax-deferred and/or tax-free retirement accounts such as those we listed above.

There is one thing certain about the volatile stock and bond markets, and that is that they will most certainly go up and come down! We cannot control or even completely mitigate this volatility of the markets. However, there are techniques we can use to help smooth out the path to our retirement goals. One such strategy is called dollar-cost averaging. This involves the discipline of purchasing a fixed dollar amount of market-driven investments on a regular basis each month regardless of what is happening to the price of that investment. Though dollar-cost averaging does not guarantee positive results, the investor does purchase more shares or units of the investment when share prices are down and fewer when they are up, just by nature of the fixed amount invested. Over the long haul, therefore, your average price per share is nearly always less than if you had tried to time the market at what you thought was the low. Another strategy to combat market volatility is simply diversifying your investments. This entails buying different types of investments, such as stocks, bonds, and real estate, in different industries, in different regions of the world, and with different maturities and in different time frames.

As far as dealing with life's unforeseen events, in the realm of retirement planning, be sure to seek the advice of professionals about having the right amount and types of life insurance, disability insurance, and long-term care or chronic illness coverages, along with adequate auto and homeowner policies with deductibles that you can handle in the event of loss.

In addition to looking at your retirement account statements regularly, don't hesitate to check your risk profile pulse. Your risk profile is how you view and respond to investment risks. Has your view of risk changed over the years? If so, you and your advisors might readjust your level of risk in your investment vehicles. A person's ideas about risk often change as they near the time for their retirement distributions to begin.

Finally, don't forget to reward yourself along the way! Yes, you should use raises and promotions to increase your retirement savings, investments, and protection plans, but it's also a good thing to choose something like a dinner out to celebrate the progress. Enjoy the journey and take time to stop, give thanks for progress, and refocus on the vision with the ones you love.

Social Security and the Blended Family[6]

At the time of the writing of this book, the Social Security Administration reported that their programs covered about one in six Americans, with around 60 million citizens receiving benefits and about 170 million workers paying Social Security taxes. Just how is the Social Security program funded for all these people?

To begin with, these numbers will change, but today's workers pay FICA taxes of 6.2 percent on up to $132,900 of annual wages (2019 figure) into the Social Security program. Funds are held in a trust fund, and benefits are paid to retirees over age sixty-two, people with disabilities, survivors of workers who died prematurely, and the spouses and children of beneficiaries. An additional 1.45–2.4 percent of a worker's income is paid into the Medicare program, based on income. Employers match those payments, so people who are self-employed pay 12.4 percent for FICA taxes and 2.9 percent to Medicare.

When a person pays into the Social Security system, they earn credits. One credit is earned for every $1,360 in wages earned in 2019, up to a maximum of four credits per year. This amount needed to earn one credit typically goes up a little bit each year. Social Security benefits are determined based upon these credits, which tie to our earnings over the years.

There are two rules within our Social Security system that reduce some benefits for those who have income from jobs that are not covered by Social Security withholding, such as some federal, state, and local government jobs or teaching positions at some public institutions.

The first rule, called the Windfall Elimination Provision, or "WEP," says that for your own Social Security retirement benefits, any pension you receive from a non-Social Security taxed position may cause a reduction to your Social Security benefits. This is to prevent "double dipping" and only applies to your own Social Security retirement benefits, not any spousal or survivor benefits.

The second rule is the Government Pension Offset, or "GPO." It applies to your spousal or survivor benefits based upon your spouse's or ex-spouse's record. These spousal or survivor Social Security benefits may be reduced up to about two-thirds of whatever the amount of your government pension that did not have Social Security taxes withheld to fund.

As with many of the Social Security program elements, the WEP and GPO rules have many variations and intricate applications, so it is recommended that you call a Social Security office or visit SocialSecurity.gov to get advice on your specific situation.

Spouses who are at least sixty-two years old, have been married twelve months or more, and have a primary benefit spouse currently taking their Social Security benefits are also eligible for spousal benefits, which total half of the spouse's benefit. This is, of course, unless the benefits based upon their own earnings record are greater. This is true even for divorced spouses as long as they were married ten years or longer, they are currently unmarried, they are at least age sixty-two, and either the former spouse is actively receiving Social Security benefits or the divorce was finalized two or more years prior to the filing date. The former spouse requesting spousal benefits must currently be unmarried.

Beth was receiving spousal benefits tied to an ex-spouse. When she remarried, those benefits ceased, which came as a big surprise to her. Now if there is a subsequent divorce or her new spouse dies, Beth once again becomes eligible for spousal benefits, as well as survivor benefits as a widow in the case of her spouse dying. In another case, Roberta had more than one former spouse whom she was married to for ten or more years. She was pleased to know that she could choose the former spouse with the highest available benefit. Roberta's former spouse has not applied for Social Security benefits yet, but she will be eligible when he does. She can receive benefit on his record because she has been divorced at least two years. If your former spouse filed before you divorced, then you do not have to wait the two years.

If you are receiving spousal benefits from a former spouse and you are planning on getting married to someone else, keep this in mind: If the person you are planning to marry is eligible for their own spousal benefits due to a divorce, have them start taking them before you marry. Many blended couples are not aware that only if you marry someone already receiving a divorced spouse benefit, or a widow(er) benefit, or benefits from mothers, fathers, or parents, can they continue their benefits when you marry. If they do not initiate payments prior to your marriage, then the marriage would stop their ability to do so. You may want to consider having both parties collecting before connecting.

If a person dies, their widow or widower is eligible to receive Social Security spousal benefits based upon the deceased spouse's earnings as long as the surviving spouse is age sixty or older and remains unmarried and the couple was married for ten or more years. If a widow(er) marries after age sixty, they retain access to the survivor benefit based upon the deceased spouse's earnings record. So in a widow's remarriage after "six-oh" the survivor benefits don't have to go.

To find more information about your contributions and eligibility to date and what you can expect in retirement, visit Social Security.gov/myaccount and create an account.

While Social Security is an important government benefit, especially as Americans are living longer, it's important to keep things in perspective. Social Security was never meant to be the primary or even the majority of retirement income. It replaces only about 40 percent of an average wage earner's income, and most financial advisors say you'll need 70–80 percent of pre-retirement earnings in retirement.

Then there are the bigger questions about the overall solvency of the Social Security program. Congress has borrowed heavily from this Social Security trust fund, and since 2010, Social Security payouts have outpaced the income and interest earned in the account. Unless something changes, Social Security principal will soon be needed to pay beneficiaries. Some experts have estimated that the Social Security trust principal will be depleted by 2033, which will require the program to be drastically altered.

So just how are our Social Security benefits calculated? There are three main factors that determine the amount of your Social Security benefits.

- Your average indexed monthly earnings (AIME), which is calculated from your highest earning thirty-five years covered by Social Security adjusted for inflation.
- Your full retirement age (FRA), which is calculated according to the year you were born (currently ages 66–67 for most). Check your account at SocialSecurity.gov/my account to determine the specific time that you are eligible for your primary insurance amount. (Your PIA is the benefit you receive when retiring at full retirement age.)
- The number of months either before or after your FRA that you decide to retire, as early as age sixty-two. Your Social Security benefit is adjusted for each month either prior to or after the FRA that you enter retirement.

Is there an ideal age to apply for Social Security retirement benefits? Once you start the application process to receive benefits, your monthly payment and your spouse's benefit payment are locked in and will only change with cost-of-living adjustments. The decision about when to start receiving payments is a very important one, and it should be part of your financial planning conversations as a couple and with your retirement planning team, also taking into account other income options like pensions, savings, investments, inheritances, businesses, and military benefits.

Here's a summary of your options: If you apply at your full retirement age, you'll receive full benefits based on the factors noted above.

George was a healthy sixty-eight-year-old, and longevity ran in his family. Having married Alkynessa, who was much younger, he wanted to get the most out of his Social Security checks for both of their lives. He discovered that if he continued to work past his FRA, up to age seventy, he would receive additional credits of 8 percent per year, with a maximum of 32 percent higher monthly payments when he retires.

In many cases, like with George and Alkynessa, if a couple doesn't need the money right away, it makes sense to delay retirement benefits until seventy, especially for the spouse with the higher earned benefits.[7] This is especially true because no more than 85 percent of Social Security is subject to taxation, while the 401(k), traditional IRAs, and other retirement plans are entirely subject to taxation. You can retire and yet still defer your decision to start taking your Social Security payments. Your financial advisor may recommend that it would be to your advantage to delay taking Social Security and instead use distributions from your retirement plan accounts to get the biggest Social Security checks later, with only 85 percent of it subject to taxation.

However, suspending or delaying benefits also suspends the benefits for your spouse and any children who are basing their potential survivor benefits on your record.

If you apply as early as possible, which is currently age sixty-two, you'll receive a reduced monthly amount, losing around half a percent for every month you retire before your FRA. So, for example, if your FRA is sixty-six years and two months, and you start receiving Social Security income at sixty-two, then your retirement checks would be 25.8 percent less than if you waited for your full retirement age. Why would someone choose that? Some people take early Social Security payments because they don't want to put off retirement, and they want the peace of mind that comes from locking in their piece of a program that may or may not be changed in the future. Others realize that they may not live long enough to take financial benefit from delayed-but-higher payments later. And then there are those who have unforeseen health issues or financial difficulties that would make earlier Social Security income necessary.

So which is best? It depends, especially when the combined Social Security benefits for a blended couple are taken into consideration. As with George and Alkynessa, you have to look at each spouse's age, life expectancy, and earning record, and then consider the spousal benefits and survivor benefits in a variety of scenarios. Your financial advisor can help you estimate the break-even age that you must live beyond in order for delayed benefits to provide a higher lifetime income. For most people, that ranges somewhere between the late seventies and about eighty years of age.

There is no percentage increase in a spouse's benefits or survivor's benefits past the FRA, so in most cases we recommend that the spouse begin taking spousal benefits as soon as the primary wage earner reaches full retirement age regardless of whether they actually retire.

One of the questions that we're often asked, especially in periods of recession, is whether a person can keep working while on Social Security retirement income. After you reach your FRA, the government allows you to work with no penalty or reduction to your Social Security benefits. However, if you have applied to start your benefits before your FRA and are also working, then there is a deduction of one dollar of benefits for every two dollars in earnings you have above a relatively small annual limit, which changes each year. In 2019, that figure was $17,640. If you are working in the year of your FRA, this reduction drops to one dollar for every three dollars earned over an annual limit that also changes.

Social Security may be taxable income depending upon your filing status, your combined income, and how much you earn while receiving payments. A helpful tool for working through this is the Retirement Earnings Test Calculator found at SSA.gov/OACT/COLA/RTeffect.html. See the same website to get up-to-date tax ramifications of Social Security payments based upon your tax filing status and your annual earnings amounts.

Big Picture: Discuss and Plan Your Next Steps

As we conclude this chapter, remember that retirement planning is a long-term journey, but one that is never too late to start on. There are many things you can do on your own, whether you are just starting or are reevaluating your retirement plan. These would include the following:

- Spend the time to envision and put in writing both your individual and blended family retirement goals.
- Take an inventory of all resources that each spouse brings to their retirement plan as these resources stand today and discuss realistic pictures of what retirement will look like.
- When you feel like you need another pair of eyes or are lacking expertise to make your retirement planning decisions on your own, seek out referrals to experienced and trusted advisors to gain wisdom and guidance.
- Make sure to coordinate all the beneficiaries of your retirement plans with your will, trusts, life insurance, and other assets with named beneficiaries.
- Review the progress of your retirement plan regularly, such as once every six months or annually. Modify the amounts and the types of vehicles as needed due to changing market conditions or changes in how you view and feel about risks. This becomes increasingly important as you get closer to the time when you will begin taking income during retirement.
- Annually review all risk-management and insurance policies that directly or indirectly protect your retirement plan. This includes both spouses' life insurance, disability insurance, and long-term care or chronic illness insurance, along with your auto and homeowners policies and possible umbrella liability coverages.
- If at all possible, as you near the ages when Social Security decisions come into focus, attempt to have a discussion with your former spouse to determine his or her benefit amount. This can help you with planning your spousal benefits. If your former spouse is deceased, then you can factor survivor benefits into your planning.

We very well may spend a third of our lives in some form of retirement. Every effort a couple makes toward retirement planning helps these years truly be the best years for blended families.

10

Planning for Healthcare Needs

William was in his early sixties, in his final few years of teaching high school and dreaming of retirement, when he got a phone call that changed his life. His wife, Denise, had had a sudden acute stroke. She was unconscious and unresponsive.

William got to the hospital at the same time as Tameka, his adult stepdaughter. The doctor pulled them both aside to explain the situation. Denise's outlook was grim; her body was being sustained with a ventilator, and it was unlikely that she would ever regain consciousness. Even if she did, the doctor warned that she would suffer severe impairments from the lack of oxygen to her brain.

"There was nothing in her file to indicate how she would want to be treated in a condition like this," the doctor told them. "So sometime soon we'll need the family to make decisions about how to proceed. Do you want us to begin artificial nutrition? Do you want every treatment available?"

William had opened his mouth to ask the doctor to do everything possible to keep his wife alive, when a tearful Tameka spoke up. "No, we can't do that to her. Mom would never want to live like that."

William looked at her. Was that true? He and Denise had never talked about what they wanted. After coming out of difficult, painful marriages, they had spent the past ten years blissfully in love and enjoying their happiness. They avoided painful conversations. But was it even Tameka's place to decide what her mom would want? Wasn't he Denise's primary family now?

More than two-thirds of American adults have not given clear instructions for how they want to be treated in medical emergencies or situations where they can't make their own decisions. For many, it's an uncomfortable topic to address, and one that's easy to put off in the middle of careers, kids, changing family dynamics, and personal needs.

But medical situations don't only happen to people who are older. Vanessa was thirty-eight, and just a few weeks shy of her third wedding anniversary, when her husband, Mike, suffered a traumatic brain injury in a car accident. Mike was left with limited speech and cognitive functions. He could no longer work, and Vanessa found herself responsible for all of the decisions related to his medical care, their finances, and their responsibilities to Mike's teenage children from his first marriage. The bills quickly started to pile up.

People in every age bracket are at risk for debilitating situations that would leave them unable to care for themselves. According to the US Department of Health and Human Services, by the time we're sixty-five, our chance of needing long-term care services to help with medical needs reaches almost 70 percent.[1] Whether it happens as the result of an accident, an illness, or the natural aging process, most of us at some point will either need care or will become a caregiver to a spouse or loved one who can no longer make decisions for themselves.

Avoiding decisions about how to handle your potential long-term medical needs doesn't make the issues go away. It only makes it harder for the people who love you and who could be left with difficult decisions and no idea how to handle them.

And the more complicated the dynamics of your blended family, the more important it is to protect the people you love by having a clear, up-to-date plan in place. Healthcare decisions that are made (or not made) in times of crisis will impact your children, extended family, spouse, and their family.

While there's no way to avoid some potential healthcare issues, there are ways to make the process smoother for everyone. As with everything, communication is key.

Step 1. Consider What You Want

Have you ever sat down and articulated what is important to you in terms of your future? Suppose tragedy happens. A stroke. An accident. A heart attack. You're rushed to the emergency room, and doctors work quickly to save you. Your spouse is in the waiting room, terribly worried, when a woman in blue scrubs comes out. "It's touch-and-go," she says. "We recommend immediate surgery, but that has serious risks, and we can't guarantee that your spouse will survive the procedure. What are your wishes?"

You may wish you were awake to make the decision for yourself, but you're not. Does your spouse know what you would want to do? Do your children, if they are old enough to make legal decisions?

Some couples have talked extensively about how to handle medical issues, but in our experience, most have not. In fact, many individuals we meet have never formally shared with the people closest to them what they would want to happen. Now is the time, while you're healthy and capable, to outline your values, your priorities, and how you want to live. While you can't predict every possible situation that might arise or provide specific instructions for every "what if" scenario, you can establish some clear guidelines of what's important to you, and your family can use them to guide their decisions in any circumstance where you aren't able to make your own decisions.

First, think about how you view your *physical life and health*. How does that affect the way you handle emergencies?

- Do you want every possible effort made to keep you alive no matter what?
- Are there situations where you would not want medical treatments (feeding tube, sedation, breathing machine, etc.) to keep you alive?
- Are there specific medical treatments you would not want?
- Are there effects of medical treatment that you would not want to experience? (For instance, if a medical procedure left you paralyzed, or permanently bedridden, or in constant pain, or unable to recognize your family and friends.)
- Who do you want to be with you or near you if you are in an extended medical situation?

It's difficult to consider these questions, and the answers might vary. Healthcare situations come with many variables—for example, needing to be on a breathing machine for a few days to fight off a case of pneumonia isn't the same as needing a breathing machine indefinitely for a condition that is not likely to resolve.

Second, consider your *financial priorities and goals*. It's no secret that medical care is expensive, and bills quickly pile up in situations where a person needs extensive care. What would your financial priorities be if you were too sick to make your own decisions? Here are some examples of what we hear most often, not necessarily in this order:

- To provide for my care.
- To provide for the care of my spouse.
- To provide for the care of my children and/or stepchildren until they become adults.
- To protect and provide an inheritance for my adult children.

- To maintain my independence, in my own home, as long as possible.
- To avoid debt that would be a burden to my family.
- To protect specific assets (real estate, family-owned business, trust fund) if possible.

You and your spouse may choose to make these decisions together, or it may be something that you each do independently and then discuss. However you approach the subject, be sure to create a written record of your wishes and priorities using the documents outlined in the following sections. Let your spouse and adult children know where you've filed these healthcare directives so that in case of emergency the person who needs to make decisions on your behalf can find them. Today, online services like DocuBank (DocuBank.com) and Legal Directives (LegalDirectives.com) provide electronic records of your healthcare directives that are accessible at any time, from anywhere in the world.

At the very least, let a few trusted family members know that you've created a file and where to find it.

Step 2. Document Your Healthcare Wishes

There are a number of forms and documents, collectively known as healthcare advance directives, that you can include in your file.

Healthcare Power of Attorney

With so many variables in healthcare and disability situations, it's impossible to consider and record your wishes for every possible outcome. That's why the single most important plan that you can make is identifying who should have the authority to make decisions for you if you can't.

Remember that scene earlier in the chapter where the doctor came into the waiting room and asked your spouse if they would consent to your surgery? Your spouse would be able to quickly

171

make that decision if you named them as your healthcare agent by signing a form called a healthcare power of attorney (POA), which is also called the healthcare directive or advance directive. Many state forms include this with a living will template so that your wishes can be conveyed directly to the person who will make decisions for you.

Your healthcare agent steps in when you can't and makes decisions about urgent situations and long-term care. They also have the legal right to request medical records, talk to a doctor or hospital about your medical options, check you in or out of a hospital, hire and fire doctors or specialists, and consent to treatment or surgery. In the final stages of life, a healthcare agent is the only person who can give the order to sustain your life by every means possible, or to stop aggressive treatment and shift to palliative care. In some instances, a state statute will allow a spouse to make emergency decisions, but in nonemergency situations, even a spouse needs the legal authority granted by a healthcare power of attorney.

For most married people, the obvious choice for healthcare agent is their spouse. But sometimes an adult child, parent, or sibling makes more sense for a specific situation. Here are some questions to ask yourself as you look at your situation.

- Do you have ongoing health issues? Is everyone in your family aware of these issues? Is there one person who regularly attends doctor visits and meetings with you? If a child or spouse has helped you face a chronic health issue for years, they may have the best understanding of the decisions you face.

- Is age a consideration? Look ahead a few years and consider where your healthcare POA[2] might be physically and mentally. If your spouse has health or memory issues, will they be equipped to focus and think clearly about important decisions? Or, on the other end of the spectrum, a child may legally be an adult (a person must be at least eighteen to be a healthcare agent), but are they prepared to tackle the life-and-death decisions that can come with being a healthcare POA?

- Does your intended healthcare POA handle stress well? If a person tends to become emotional and overwhelmed in stressful situations, will they be able to make tough decisions quickly when needed? Are they naturally a peacemaker and able to communicate and include the rest of your loved ones?

- Does this person share your values, or at least respect your choices about how you want things handled? If you and they fundamentally disagree on sensitive issues like end-of-life care, do you trust them to make the decision you want in that situation?

- Can they be a good advocate for you? Good medical care often requires the patient or the power of attorney to ask good questions and be proactive in seeking out the proper treatment or course of action. Someone who is naturally passive or agreeable may have a hard time standing up to doctors, or other loved ones.

- If you are considering someone other than a spouse, does that person live close enough to respond in case of emergency?

If you have not designated an agent through a power of attorney and something happens to you, your family will have to go to court and ask a judge to appoint a guardian. It's a time-consuming and expensive process, and not something that a family should have to go through while also juggling stressful issues.

Do Not Resuscitate (DNR)/POLST and Living Wills

While your healthcare POA will have final authority in making decisions, there are some standard documents that you can keep on file to make your own wishes and priorities clear. The first is a DNR, which stands for "do not resuscitate." In many states, this is often now called a POLST, which stands for "practitioner orders for life-sustaining treatment." It is a standardized form that must be signed by a doctor or practitioner and is usually kept in a patient's medical and hospital files.

The specific language varies somewhat from state to state, but the DNR/POLST generally addresses what kinds of treatments you want in a medical emergency where you cannot communicate; specifically, if necessary whether you want a ventilator, a feeding tube, or to be revived with CPR if your heart stops. The options vary from "full treatment" (all procedures available and appropriate to keep a patient alive) to "limited treatment" (basic medical treatment but not mechanical ventilation) to "comfort measures only" (maximizing comfort through symptom management). It will also ask whether you want artificially administered nutrition and hydration if you are unable to eat or drink.

If you are checking into a hospital for an elective surgery or other procedure, the medical staff may ask if you have a living will. A living will is another type of form that states your general wishes regarding end-of-life treatment and whether you want to be kept alive by "extraordinary measures." This is a legally binding document, but it serves as a backup to your healthcare power of attorney. As long as you have a POA, the living will document primarily provides confirmation and guidance about how you would want things handled.

Very few people complete a DNR/POLST when they are young and relatively healthy, when they have a reasonable expectation that lifesaving procedures like CPR could bring them back to a high quality of life. However, a DNR/POLST is an extremely valuable tool for those facing advanced age or serious health problems where lifesaving treatments may provide minimal extension of life and perhaps no quality of life.

If you don't already have a DNR/POLST in place, your healthcare POA can add one. They can also change your DNR/POLST, cancel it, or reinstate it. They will also have the final say in what "extraordinary measures" are appropriate in a specific situation.

Step 3. Document Your Financial Wishes

Legally, there are two separate areas where a person can step in if someone is incapacitated, disabled, or otherwise unable to care for themselves. The first is medical care decisions, which we've discussed. But the second is a need for a person to handle financial decisions if someone is unable to do it for themselves. Many casually refer to this as "taking over the checkbook," but it actually encompasses a great amount of responsibility and power.

Many of the people we talk to don't realize that the right to make financial decisions for another person is not automatically granted, even to a spouse or adult child. And in a blended family, where the dynamics among family members and loved ones may be complicated, it is particularly important to designate whom you wish to be responsible for different aspects of your care, and to communicate that decision to everyone involved. Even if you hope that your loved ones—your spouse, parents, adult children, siblings, etc.—will make important decisions together, legally there must be one person with final decision-making power. That person is free to discuss their options with anyone they like (family, friends, doctors, clergy), but their decisions stand even if other family members disagree.

There are two primary legal documents that can help you plan for this part of your financial future.

Revocable Living Trust

Think of a revocable living trust as a book with different chapters. It outlines your instructions for your estate in case of your death or incapacitation. The revocable living trust is legally binding and can convey your wishes on anything from how your finances should be handled after your death to who should make important decisions if you are unable to do so for yourself. If you have dependent children, you can leave instructions about their care and financial support. Be sure to discuss this with an attorney, who may suggest more specific documents depending on your situation.

There are four important questions to consider and address in your plan for disability.

How should your family or medical providers decide whether you are unable to make decisions for yourself? How should your family determine when it's time to take your checkbook (or online banking login) and car keys away? Your revocable trust can include guidelines for when you want those decisions to be made, such as when you're making poor decisions to the detriment of yourself or others. Ultimately, a person's competence is decided by a doctor or medical practitioner, but there are often gray areas of vulnerability when a person may not be medically unsound but still isn't capable of reasonably handling their own affairs. An accident or health emergency may suddenly leave you with limited capacity, or creeping age could change your cognitive and physical abilities gradually. Perhaps you've seen this in a parent or neighbor. Most of us know a person who is clearly slipping, though they believe they're fine.

Who should decide to take your checkbook or keys? Is there one person whom you trust to evaluate your capacity to care for yourself, like a family physician? Would you prefer to designate a group of trusted friends and advisors? Many people today designate what's called a disability panel of four or five people, which might include family members as well as more objective observers like neighbors, pastors, attorneys, or close friends. If you designate a disability panel, you can also decide whether a majority vote or unanimous vote is required to take away your financial power.

Who should handle your affairs if you are unable to? If you're not in a position to make decisions for yourself, who should have the legal authority to act for you in financial matters? This person is often referred to as your disability trustee. They will probably be a member of your disability panel if you have one, because they are one of your most trusted people. To avoid a conflict of interest, though, the disability trustee shouldn't have the sole authority to evaluate your capacity and should be subject to the guidelines for a majority or unanimous vote. We'll talk about this more in the next section.

Once the disability trustee takes over your money, how do you want things handled? A revocable trust is your opportunity to leave instructions and guidelines. For instance, does your disability trustee have permission to mortgage or sell your property or go into debt in your name in order to pay for medical care? Are there regular donations to churches or charities that should be maintained, if possible? If your adult children have financial needs, do you want your funds to be available to help them during your disability?

Durable Power of Attorney

A person appointed as your durable power of attorney (along with your disability trustee, if you have one) will handle your day-to-day responsibilities if you are incapacitated. They'll pay your bills, file your insurance claims and tax returns, invest your money, handle any maintenance or repair expenses in your home, sell your property, manage your bank accounts, and on and on. A durable power of attorney can even legally borrow money on your behalf.

In our experience, most people assign durable power of attorney to the same person who is also listed as their disability trustee, so that they can handle any financial matters that come up, using whichever legal document they need in a situation.

There's little legal oversight over a power of attorney's actions and choices beyond a general requirement that they do everything for the benefit of the person they represent, so you can see why it's a critical decision to make in advance of any debilitating condition. Once the POA is established, the choice should be reviewed regularly, along with the other details in your living trust.

A durable power of attorney does not need to be the same person as the healthcare power of attorney, although he or she can be. Younger couples and those without serious health concerns often grant all of the decision-making rights to their spouse. Aging couples, or those marrying later in life, sometimes choose a child to make financial decisions instead of a spouse. Some consider options other than spouse or children, such as an experienced professional who can act objectively without emotion and family pressure. Options like a bank, trust company, CPA, or attorney could be named to handle financial issues, while personal health-care decisions are still entrusted to family members. You may also look at your family and intuitively know that one person will be better equipped to make healthcare decisions under stress and time constraints, while another is a better long-term manager of resources.

Step 4. Plan Financially for Disability or Long-Term Care

Long-term care for aging or disability can come in many forms. You might need to pay for care at home, live in a retirement or assisted living community, or depend on a skilled nursing facility or nursing home.

Do you have the financial resources to cover the costs of that kind of long-term disability or need for care? Probably not.

While advances in health and medicine have done a remarkable job of extending our lives, they've also come with a significant cost. As we mentioned before, almost 70 percent of Americans entering their senior years will need long-term care at some point. Twenty percent will need such care for more than five years, according to the Department of Health and Human Services.[3] When a single month of medical care can cost $5,000, $10,000, or even more in some states, the numbers add up quickly.

The more you plan ahead, the more options and resources will be available if and when you need them, and the more your family will be able to carry out your wishes.

Broadly speaking, there are five ways that most people pay for long-term medical care.

1. **Use your income.** In an ideal situation, there is enough money coming in to cover the expenses. Income might include work compensation (if a spouse is still working), Social Security, a pension, investment dividends or interest, property income, etc.

2. **Use your assets.** You may need to tap in to your savings, IRA, house equity, investments, CDs, property, etc.

3. **Use insurance.** In addition to owning regular health insurance, families can lighten their potential future burden by purchasing private insurance that covers disability and long-term care. It's important to point out that these are two different kinds of insurance: Disability insurance[4] replaces some portion of your income if you are unable to work but does not directly cover costs for your care. Most people who are employed by others have disability insurance through their employer. Long-term care insurance is not based on employment or income, but on health needs. Most policies cover daily-living services like bathing, dressing, or feeding if policyholders need them at some point in the future. Good long-term care policies, purchased either separately or in conjunction with health or even life insurance, cover in-home care as well as care in assisted living and nursing facilities.

For most younger blended families, disability insurance will cover your immediate needs in case of an emergency. But as you age, long-term care becomes a more important consideration. Traditional long-term care insurance is a "use it or lose it" policy, much like car or health insurance. A person pays premiums, probably for years, on the chance that they will someday need to use the service. If you are part of the 30 percent of seniors who never need care, the premiums you paid aren't refundable.

Another insurance option is called hybrid long-term coverage. In this, a person purchases and pays premiums (either monthly or a onetime lump sum premium) on a life insurance policy or annuity. Attached to the policy, though, is a long-term care rider that gives the policyholder the right to access their benefit amount if they need funds for their care. If they do not use long-term care, all of the money goes to their beneficiary at their death.

4. Use VA benefits if you are a wartime veteran. If you are a military veteran who served during wartime, you may qualify for a Veterans Pension after you turn sixty-five to help pay for care. This benefit is often called Aid and Attendance. To qualify, you must demonstrate that you need daily care and help with at least two "activities of daily living" such as eating, bathing, dressing, or toileting. VA benefits cover care provided at home, in an assisted living facility, or in a skilled nursing facility. The surviving spouse of a wartime veteran may also access this benefit.

The only downside to this benefit is that government bureaucracies are notoriously complicated. To qualify for the maximum benefit, it's a good idea to seek guidance from an experienced elder law attorney who is accredited with the Veterans Administration.

5. Use Medicaid benefits. This federally funded program pays the largest share of the costs associated with long-term care. Many families see it as a last resort because a person must meet certain income and state eligibility requirements, which almost always specify that a patient must first deplete their own resources.

This creates a number of challenges that are particularly relevant to blended families, because the government considers all of the assets of a married couple when determining Medicaid eligibility. This is true even if you and your spouse maintain separate accounts or own property or a business that's being held for a future generation. The law, as written, is inflexible, and not even a prenuptial agreement can protect individual assets.

However, with proper advance planning, you or your spouse could access Medicaid benefits to care for immediate physical needs while still protecting specific assets, like your house, for the other spouse or your children. A good lawyer can help you analyze your situation and develop a Medicaid qualification strategy to get needed support before all of your funds are "spent down" on care. Some families can protect as much as 50–90 percent of their assets while still obtaining the medical care that they need.

The key to all of this, of course, is communication. All the legal and financial planning in the world can be undone if a family is unclear about what your wishes are, or if there is disagreement or conflict among your loved ones.

Be open with your spouse, your children, and your extended family about your plans and desires. Let them know that you have made formal plans and ask for their support in following your wishes as much as possible if and when the time comes.

As we said earlier in the chapter, consider digitizing these documents and uploading them to the cloud in a safe and secure location. Many companies offer such services. Giving a trusted family member access allows them to find these crucial documents in case of an urgent need.

Surprises might be fun when there are birthdays or presents involved, but they can be tragic when families are dealing with the stress and burden of a loved one's illness and trying to make wise decisions.

11

Planning Your Estate

When was the last time you reviewed your will? Do you have one?

If you don't have a will, you're not alone. According to a 2016 Gallup poll, less than half of all Americans have a written plan for how to handle their estate after their death, and that number drops to about one-third among those between thirty and fifty years old.[1]

There are serious consequences to dying without a plan in place, though. If a person passes away without a will, the division of their assets is determined according to their state's probate laws. After the deceased's debts are paid, remaining assets are distributed according to the state's formula for defining the next of kin. For a blended family, that usually means set percentages are distributed to the surviving spouse and the deceased's biological and legally adopted children. There is no flexibility in the strict rules of a probate court to consider the intricacies of a blended family situation.

This is a difficult process for a grieving family to have to endure, and it can add at least a year of financial and emotional stress to an already difficult situation, not to mention expensive legal fees and possibly a higher tax bill.

However, in our experience even some families who think they have made an estate plan may not be fully protected or prepared.

For example, consider Elizabeth. When Elizabeth had her first child, she and her husband did all of the responsible financial things. They bought life insurance, opened a college savings account, and wrote their wills, designating Elizabeth's parents as the guardians of their son and the trustees for whatever assets they could scrape together for his care and education. Elizabeth mentally checked the box that she had "planned for the future."

That was nineteen years ago. Since then, Elizabeth and her husband have divorced. Through her new job with the county government, she opened a retirement account and started to tuck a little money away for the future. A few years later she married André, who moved into her house, and they had two more children. Her oldest son went off to college. Her father passed away, and her mother moved out of state.

During those busy years, Elizabeth didn't think about the papers in her safe-deposit box. She was too busy trying to manage a hectic, challenging present. But when an acquaintance was diagnosed with cancer and given a dire prognosis, Elizabeth started to wonder about her own situation. What would happen to her family if she wasn't around?

When she read the will she'd written long ago, Elizabeth was horrified to discover how out-of-date it was. Not only was her mom no longer healthy enough to care for a bunch of active kids, but there was no reference to André anywhere. Her former husband was still listed as the beneficiary of her life insurance policy!

Elizabeth's situation is not unique. We know of quite a few divorced spouses who were surprised to discover that their ex unintentionally left them an inheritance through a forgotten insurance policy or investment account. Even more families find that their grief over an unexpected loss is interrupted by complications of untangling an estate left with confusing instructions or, even worse, no instructions at all.

That's what happened to Samantha. She was Jason's second wife and significantly younger than him. They were deeply in love and had been married for more than a decade when Jason died suddenly of a heart attack at just sixty-five.

Jason had encouraged her to quit her job in human relations so that they could enjoy his retirement together. His house was paid for, and the generous stock package he had received from his former employer would be more than enough to provide for Samantha for the rest of her life, he assured her.

But when the family sat down to go through Jason's will and assets, they discovered he'd never formally updated his estate plan. He still listed his adult children as his only account beneficiaries, and a trust left them his house. Two weeks later, Jason's son told Samantha that the family was putting the house on the market and she needed to move out within the week. At almost fifty, she was left with nowhere to live and few resources.

Now, if something happened to you tomorrow, your kids hopefully wouldn't turn out their stepparent like Jason's did. But blended families are complicated, and life can often feel like a series of exercises in balancing the needs and desires of your spouse and your children. Estate planning will likely be one of those times.

If the healthcare planning we did in the previous chapter is life planning, then thinking about your estate is, by definition, death planning. That's a hard topic to think about. In the rush of day-to-day responsibilities, it's easy to put it off. But whether we're ready or not, death is something that each of us will eventually face. The best gift we can give our loved ones is an organized, well-documented plan for how we want them to proceed.

When it comes to something as significant and sensitive as sorting through a legacy, it's not a good idea to just assume, "It will all work out without me." Instead, set aside time as a couple to research and reflect as well as to make and document some tough decisions.

What Are Your Assets?

Unless you have a lot of money and possessions to spread around, you may not have considered yourself as a person with an estate. Estate is just a term that describes all of the things that a person leaves behind when they die. Everyone has one. Even if your kids are grown and all you have is a mortgaged house, a barely there checking account, and an old car, you have an estate that needs to be handled.

Billions of dollars of unclaimed property, from abandoned bank accounts to unclaimed insurance payments, are turned over to state governments every year. Many of these are accounts lost in estate transitions. To avoid this, and to make sure that your loved ones receive everything you've set aside for them, create a single file with a list (an "own and owe" list as discussed in appendix 2) of all your accounts, policies, and valuable assets. Do you have IRAs from old employers? Savings bonds tucked away? Pension fund paperwork or a life insurance policy?

Make sure there is a paper copy of the list that is easily accessible to those who will eventually need it. Creating your own organized record of assets is especially important today, when financial statements are often only delivered electronically and physical paper trails are virtually nonexistent.

Once you have a complete list, identify any assets that are jointly owned with your spouse or other family members. This includes any bank account, title, or real estate deed that lists more than one name as co-owners. What you brought into your marriage, from your savings account to the ugly leather couch in the basement, is considered your sole possession unless you have specifically added your spouse's name to the title or deed. It does not matter how long you've jointly lived in a house or driven a car, or whether anyone other than the title holder contributed financially.

If you die before your spouse, your joint assets will automatically transfer to them. Any account or policy that lists someone else as a co-owner or a beneficiary will automatically transfer to them. This is why it is important to regularly review those files. The first time you set up a life insurance policy you had to provide instructions for where the funds should be directed in case of your death. Savings accounts, money markets, or certificates of deposit may also have a "payable on death" beneficiary listed. No matter how long ago you made that choice, or what life changes have happened since, that designation will supersede anything you say in a will, trust, or other document. So if there are any accounts that need to be redirected, make that your top priority.

Some of your accounts or assets may have automatic beneficiary designations that cannot be changed. If you have a pension, for example, it will probably continue to pay a surviving spouse and then cancel on the spouse's death. With Social Security, the government will adjust the surviving spouse's income to account for any difference in monthly payment.

Retirement accounts—whether 401(k)s, IRAs, or annuities— are each handed differently. Read the paperwork carefully and talk to your financial advisor or an estate lawyer to understand how the beneficiary process works, including what happens if you fail to name a beneficiary or if your beneficiary is deceased.

While you're organizing records, this is also a good time to make a list of any outstanding debts you might owe. Is there a mortgage on the house? Did you take out personal equity loans to pay for your daughter's college tuition? When a person dies, their personal debt (credit card debt, student loans, mortgages, car loans, etc.) must be paid from the assets in their estate before any money can be transferred to an heir. However, assets that have an assigned beneficiary and those that are protected in pensions or certain retirement accounts are often protected from creditors. A creditor cannot come after your family for payment after the estate is emptied. In the event that a person's debt is larger than their assets, the debt "dies with them."

What Is Most Important to You?

Now that you have a clear picture of your assets, the next step is to consider what you want those resources to accomplish: Who do you want to give to, what do you want them to receive, and when do you want them to receive it?

That's simple. I want my family to be cared for and comfortable, you might think. But what does that really look like? Many families we meet assume that if one spouse dies, everything will automatically be given to the surviving spouse, and then after that person passes away, the remaining assets will be split among their children. But real life can be more complicated, especially in blended family situations.

Consider that the average American lives to be almost eighty. How old will your children be when your spouse is eighty? Do you want them to wait until their own retirement years to receive their legacy from you? And what if your spouse remarries? Are you comfortable with them bringing your inheritance into that new relationship? What if your daughter, who has a history of being irresponsible with money and men, ends up getting divorced or sued? Would your hard-earned money end up with an ex-spouse or a creditor?

It's hard to imagine some of those things now, but perspectives and relationships can change over time. For example, consider Carra and Alex. They were married for ten happy years, and together they raised Carra's daughter, Emma, from a previous relationship. When Carra was diagnosed with an aggressive cancer at just forty-five, Alex promised he would always provide for Emma. Carra passed away a year later, when Emma was just thirteen. The girl went to live with her biological father.

Carra's will left all of her assets to Alex, including the house that she'd bought before they met. At first, Alex stayed in touch with his stepdaughter, but when Emma moved away for college, and then her first job, they drifted apart. She never asked for financial help, and he never offered. Ten years after Carra's death,

Alex remarried and sold the house. He used the profits to buy a new home with his new wife, which became their joint property. Emma never received a penny.

Alex's actions were perfectly legal. A person can rewrite their own will, redirect their assets, and change their estate plan at any time, regardless of the verbal agreements they might have made with someone who predeceased them.

That's why estate planning requires long-term thinking. We hope that you, your spouse, and your children will all live full and happy lives for many decades to come, and your plan should reflect that same hope. However, a tragedy like cancer can occur at a young age, so you need to consider that the surviving spouse may live many more years.

So, with a long-term view in mind, articulate your specific priorities. What is most important for you to accomplish? What else would you like to do if it's financially possible?

Every family's situation is different, but here are some examples.

- I want my spouse to have everything that I have, because we earned it together.
- I want my spouse to be safe and comfortable for the rest of their life.
- I want my spouse to be provided for throughout the rest of their life, or until they remarry.
- I want to protect my family legacy (a family-owned business, real estate passed down through generations, etc.) and make sure my kids get it.
- I want to make sure my kids can pay for their educations/ first homes/student loans/weddings/children's needs.
- I want to make sure my child with special needs will be cared for as long as they live.
- I want each of my closest family members to have something special from me to show them that I love them.
- I want to leave a gift to my church or favorite charity.

There's no right answer to any of this, because every family situation is different. Your priorities will depend on the size and age of your family, the agreements and understandings you have with your spouse and children, and the size and structure of your estate. Couples who enter marriage later in life, each spouse bringing their own assets, will likely have different priorities than a couple who marries with very few material assets and grows together.

Also, as couples age and children move out of the house, the balance of priorities might shift. If your spouse is working or has an income of their own, your estate plan will probably be different than if they are entirely dependent on your salary, investments, or retirement income.

For most couples in blended families, the biggest, hardest decisions about estate planning come down to how to balance the needs of your spouse and your kids. There are really four options.

1. *All or nothing.* Leave it all to your spouse or all to your kids. But this could leave one side lacking, so some families consider other options.

2. *Split it up.* Some assets go to the spouse, some to the kids. Perhaps the house or IRA money goes to the spouse, and the life insurance money goes to the kids.

3. *Timing.* As we discussed in Carra and Alex's situation, what if the spouse stays in the house as long as they want and then sells it and the money goes to the children? Or what about savings or investments? Maybe the income goes to the spouse during their life and then the accounts go to the children.

4. *Increase the pot.* What if you lack enough resources to meet all the needs of both spouse and children? Some blended families purchase life insurance policies that will increase the funds available. This is something that even a family with modest income and assets can consider, because term life insurance policies for young and even middle-aged adults are generally affordable.

How Will You Communicate Your Plan?

The two primary documents that record a person's legally binding final wishes are a will, also known as a last will and testament, and a revocable living trust, which we introduced in the last chapter.

Revocable living trusts cover a number of different topics, from handling disability and long-term care while you're still alive to communicating your values and hopes for your family's future after your death. In terms of estate planning, the most important purpose of a trust is to hold assets or property for the benefit of others.

A trust not only directs what assets should be set aside for a specific heir, but can also provide instructions for the disbursement, the timing of the disbursement, and the spending approval process for those funds. Money or property that is secured in a trust is separated from the bulk of your estate and can be protected from creditors and any future family changes or concerns, including your spouse's or children's future marriages and divorces, legal trouble, or unwise spending.

Establishing a trust gives you a level of control over your assets that extends past the initial disbursement. Trusts give you the option to include fluid instructions, like stipulating a schedule on which your children will receive funds from the inheritance as they get older, or specific things (like education) that they can use the funds for. If a trust is large enough, it can provide income to a spouse for as long as they live, without transferring the ownership of the account itself. When the spouse dies, the trust dictates how the remainder of the assets is directed.

When most people think about estate planning, though, they don't think about revocable trusts. They think about **wills**, the more widely known and focused document that specifically expresses your final wishes for the breadth of your property and estate. If it is properly witnessed, even the most informal will is legally binding—although, as we saw earlier, the desires expressed in a will don't supersede beneficiary designations attached to specific accounts.

191

If your children are not yet eighteen years old, one of the most important things your will does is to assign guardians who will become responsible for them in a situation where both parents are deceased or have terminated parental rights. Depending on your estate plan, your will may also name the trustees who will help manage your children's inheritance.

Do you have specific items you want to make sure go to certain loved ones? Perhaps you know your brother will care for and continue to restore the classic car in your garage, or you want your daughter to have her grandmother's wedding china. A will assigns personal property and assets beyond the joint assets or those with designated beneficiaries. This may include personal bank accounts, investments, property, and any "special stuff," such as photo scrapbooks, family heirlooms, or jewelry. How you divide these things is entirely up to you. Anything that's not specifically designated in your will is considered part of the general estate, and your executor, whom we'll discuss in the next section, will have the authority as to its sale or distribution.

An estate attorney familiar with the laws of your state can help you draft a will that will meet your specific priorities and family needs. It may be tempting to use one of the inexpensive or free templates available online to create a basic will, but you'll need to balance the immediate cost savings with the drawbacks of using a generic form that may not reflect your specific situation or family structure, not to mention your values, goals, or concerns.

As we said earlier, anything that's vague or unclear in an estate can lead to court costs, legal battles, and hurt feelings. Over the years, many estate lawyers make more money cleaning up the estate messes of families without a clear plan than they do helping others plan ahead while they're still healthy. You are better off, both financially and emotionally, spending the time, energy, and money now to set up a plan that works. An estate attorney will help you create a complete estate plan that protects the inheritance you're leaving from probate court interference, burdensome taxes, and, to some extent, human complications.

Remember the example from earlier in the chapter about Carra, the woman whose daughter never received anything from her mom's estate? An attorney could have helped Carra structure her estate differently so that both her spouse and her child were cared for.

Here are two example scenarios:

- Carra could have set aside some of her assets, including her house, in a trust in her daughter's name, with specific instructions that Alex could live there for as long as he wanted, as long as he paid the property taxes and maintenance expenses. If he ever sold the house, the proceeds would be split between him and Emma.

- Or, if Carra had a life insurance policy, she could have designated that the proceeds for that be put into a trust for her daughter to inherit when she reached a certain age or stage of life and then left the entire house to Alex.

Who Will Execute Your Plan?

Just as your healthcare plan depends largely on making sure that there is a trusted and responsible person to act on your behalf, your estate plan also hinges on whom you choose to be your helper and legal representative. Every estate needs an executor, the person appointed in your will to be responsible for seeing that your wishes are carried out. Your executor will make sure that any outstanding bills are paid, assets are gathered and assigned, claims and tax returns are filed, and your personal property is appropriately distributed according to your wishes.

The role of an executor is to carry out the instructions left in your will. Ideally, you will leave instructions that are so clear that there are few questions about what should happen. However, executors always have some discretion in dealing with the nuts and bolts of a will. For instance, if your house is to be sold, there are still questions about which Realtor to use, what listing price to ask, whether to upgrade the house before selling, etc.

If you have established a trust as part of your estate plan, you will also need to assign a trustee.

The trustee will protect the assets until your children are old enough to inherit, or they will manage an investment account where the interest is supporting your surviving spouse. While the responsibilities of the executor of a will are relatively time limited, a trustee's role may last much longer, spreading over years or even decades.

As we saw in the last chapter, trustees generally operate under a set of guidelines to work in the best interest of the beneficiary but also have some leeway as time passes and circumstances change. For example, a trustee may have the latitude to decide whether a child beneficiary can take extra money from their fund in order to cover costs from a health emergency or buy a new car.

An estate executor or trustee may be a professional with experience in estate law, like an attorney, or even a bank, or it may be a family member or even a trusted close friend. There are costs involved in naming a professional, but there's also reassurance of proper management and smart investments. Their role in your personal life isn't as important as their ability to do the job well.

Here are a few questions to ask as you consider who should be responsible for your final wishes:

1. **Is the person ready to handle the job?** They don't have to be an expert in law, accounting, or investments. However, they will be overseeing legal and financial issues, so it's best if they aren't intimidated by those things. They may need to get help from lawyers, accountants, and financial advisors. Will that be overwhelming for them?

2. **Can you trust the person to make good decisions?** Only in rare cases does someone actually steal from an estate or trust. Far more often, a well-intentioned person makes poor decisions or makes no decisions at all. If your family member doesn't handle their own money wisely, it may

not be a good idea to hand them the checkbook to a trust fund. If they tend to be high-spirited and argumentative, consider whether they will be able to put aside their own feelings to act as a peacemaker if required; handling your estate and the needs and desires of different people will require a certain amount of tact.

3. **Will the person be placed in a difficult family situation by becoming the decision maker?** This can happen when a sibling has to make decisions for another sibling or a stepchild is put in charge of managing their stepmother's trust. Will the job duties cause conflict or even a broken relationship for the person you choose?

4. **How often will the person need to be involved?** Are there aspects of your estate that require ongoing attention or that might be time consuming? This could be anything from ongoing management of an active trust fund that's providing living costs to sorting through household goods and selling property. If your executor has a full plate of professional and family obligations, will they be able to manage your affairs in a timely fashion?

5. **Is the person nearby?** If not, does it matter? In many cases, an executor or trustee who lives out of state can handle all of the responsibilities of the estate, especially if the documentation and instructions are clear and files are well organized. But if your estate will include things that must be done in person—for example, sorting personal property and belongings in a large house—the travel requirements may create a burden.

You can also name more than one person to be co-executors or co-trustees, requiring that they work together. That adds a level of accountability but also can make the process less efficient. And if they can't agree, then the probate court will have to step in to settle the dispute, costing more time and money.

Does Your Family Know Your Plan?

If something tragic happened and your family needed to pull out your plan, would they know whom to call and what to do? Would they be surprised, hurt, or disappointed by anything they discovered?

We've all watched the scene in the movie or TV show where a shocking surprise is revealed at the public reading of a person's will. In reality, the law doesn't require a reading of the will, but there can still be plenty of stress and drama in private. The single most important thing you can do to bless your family in a difficult time, and to prevent any unnecessary tension and expense, is to make sure you're not leaving behind any big surprises.

As part of your formal estate planning, communicate about your decisions and actions with the appropriate family members. At the very least, talk to your spouse and the person or people you've selected to be the guardians, executors, and trustees after your death. Make sure that they know where you keep your will, asset list, and account information.

If you've had to make difficult decisions and you anticipate hurt feelings, consider whether you need to address your decisions with those people directly. We have had many clients write letters to explain their reasons or intentions regarding their wishes. These letters could be given to family now, or perhaps only after your passing. Such letters can not only help clarify wishes and reasons, but can be very meaningful because they contain the deepest thoughts and dreams of the deceased person.

How Often Should You Review Your Plan?

Life is always changing. Your family expands through marriage or birth and contracts through divorce or death. Your assets expand with a new retirement account, or contract when the stock market sinks or a property is sold. You move, marry, retire, and grieve. In a blended family, all of those connections can be exponentially complicated.

196

Once a year, make a date with your spouse to sit down and review your estate plan. Have you added or closed any accounts or made any major purchases that affect your asset list? Have there been any major life changes in your family that would affect whom you name as beneficiaries or as helpers?

Most years, this review will take less than an hour. But those few minutes now are a gift that your family will thank you for later. After all, estates aren't just about bank accounts and income. They're also about security and personal memories.

Depending on your age and the size or complexity of your estate, you should also meet with your estate attorney for a professional review of the material every two or three years, or any time there is a major life change like a marriage, move, or new child. An estate attorney can help you keep your legal instructions up-to-date as well as make sure your asset ownership and beneficiary designations are set up properly and in line with any changes in the laws or tax rules.

From the antique pedal sewing machine that your mother used to make her wedding dress, to the house that you and your spouse now share, to the savings account you've set aside for your youngest child's college education, your estate is the final gift you leave your family to show them how important they are. Being willing to think ahead and organize yourself to ensure the smoothest, most supportive outcome for your family is one of the kindest and most generous things you can do for the people you love.

12

Stay Calm and Stay the Course

Serena found what she described to her friends as "the man of her dreams." He had one son; she had a boy and a girl. What she didn't know—and he didn't tell her—was that he was $20,000 in debt to his former wife for back child support and alimony and was in contempt of court.

Dante's parents divorced when he was young, and his father soon married. He and his stepmother tolerated each other, while he and his father were very close. When his father became seriously ill, Dante and his dad revisited the financial promises he had made to Dante, but it was only after he died that Dante discovered his dad never documented them legally. Dante's stepmother had control over everything and refused to fulfill her husband's verbal commitments.

Marcella signed a prenup before her second marriage. Her fiancé had accumulated a fair amount of wealth and owned two businesses. She knew she wasn't marrying him for his money, so when he asked if she'd sign an agreement, she immediately said yes. But she wasn't prepared for the feeling of humiliation she experienced as she walked into the lawyer's office. It felt like he was telling everyone he didn't trust her and needed to protect himself. Over time, Marcella started to consider the prenup as a symbol of his selfishness. "I have definitely put up a wall," she said. "Now I don't trust him."

These stories reveal what dishonesty, selfishness, and poor financial planning can do to a marriage and family. But even in the absence of these detrimental actions, well-intentioned people can struggle to merge their financial lives. Bringing together the above-the-surface financial matters of a blended family with below-the-surface relational dynamics is not an easy task for most people, and, frankly, it's flat-out challenging for some. It seems there is risk, emotional and financial, at every turn.

But if your relational and financial merging process is glued together by the bonds of commitment, honesty, and integrity, you can endure risk and imperfect moments and merge your family.

Galen was a thirty-something divorced teacher with three children under ten who lived in another state. Jada was in her late twenties, did not have children, and was just launching her profession. He brought some debt into their marriage, while she brought a promising career at an investment firm and her personal discipline as a saver.

They made a Togetherness Agreement and agreed to merge all of their financial resources and income into one checking and one savings account. The merger between stepmom and stepchildren went well too; she soon fell in love with Galen's kids, and with only a few apprehensions they also welcomed her into their lives.

Because Galen's kids lived three hundred miles away, visitation was financially costly and required careful planning. For the first few years of their marriage, the couple made the four-and-a-half-hour drive on a regular basis, spent two nights in a hotel, and returned home. The two days spent in a hotel brought many memorable adventures but had many challenges as well. The weekends were not cheap, but Galen and Jada valued the time, budgeted for it, and made it work.

Over time, they added three more children to their family. Each transition and developmental stage required the couple to again negotiate their financial plans in light of their blended family's progress. For the most part, they agreed on the big stuff like cars, college, and computers, but not always.

Once, while Jada was visiting relatives out of state, Galen decided to purchase a vehicle without her knowledge. They already had a family minivan, so he rationalized buying a two-seat Porsche 911. He hid the car in the garage to surprise her when she returned home. When the garage door opened, her disapproval was evident. "Where are the kids going to sit?" she asked. (Though it certainly wasn't funny at the time, this would later become a humorous catchphrase they both used to express disapproval of either a financial or relational circumstance.)

They tried their best to treat "his" children and "theirs" equally. But finding fair wasn't always easy. Three of the children had another household contributing to their college expenses. And when one child opted to attend a two-year technical program and another took a full seven years to get a liberal arts degree after changing schools and majors twice, they often wondered if they had been equally considerate of everyone.

Now, after thirty years together and many lessons learned, the couple and family celebrate their relational and financial investments in each other. Mistakes were made, but commitment, forgiveness, and the willingness to take risks together have resulted in significant dividends. They stayed the course and, at every bend in the road, financed togetherness.

To help you obtain financial security, investment experts—who are addressing your financial bottom line—use phrases like:

- invest over an extended period of time;
- during market stress, endure ups and downs with perseverance;
- risk is necessary for reward;
- leverage your resources;

201

- don't overextend yourself—live within your means;
- plan for the future, but keep it simple; and
- expect uncertainty and unknowns, but stay calm and stay the course.

We suggest you do the same across the relational domains of your family to finance marital togetherness and achieve blended family security. Invest in one another, and especially invest in your marriage. When relationships are under stress, endure the ups and downs with perseverance and determination. Take calculated risks to merge your financial and emotional worlds so you can leverage your relational equity toward the future. Create trust in one another even as you establish financial trusts. And expect uncertainty and unknowns in your marriage and blended family—there are many dynamics, factors, and circumstances you cannot control. But stay calm and stay the course, and your investment will pay off.

Appendix 1

Pension Options Case Study

James's pension at Bigg Lumber and Supply Co. requires him to work for twenty years in order to be vested. When he and Keesha started to plan their wedding, he had only been with the company for seven years. When James looked out thirteen more years and calculated his pension options, he implemented a technique that really maximized Keesha's financial future. His company pension at Bigg Lumber and Supply Co. offered him these three options at age sixty:

- Life Only Option, where James receives the maximum available $2,000 per month, but Keesha would receive nothing after James's death.
- Joint and 50 Percent Survivor Option, where James receives $1,600 per month, and Keesha would receive $800 per month after James's death.
- Joint and 100 Percent Survivor Option, where James gets $1,400 per month, and Keesha would continue to get $1,400 per month at James's death.

After discussing all the pros and cons with their financial advisor, James and Keesha decided to select the Life Only Option above.

At first glance you might say, "What! That cuts Keesha completely out of any survivor income!" This is true. However, with Keesha's permission and signature, and with James's health good enough, he first qualified for a $350,000 death benefit universal life insurance policy. This policy only costs James about $450 per month to purchase now, which is less than the $600 per month drop in residual income from the Joint and 100 Percent Survivor Option of $1,400. Assuming that it is guaranteed and that Keesha owns it, this $350,000 policy at a guaranteed 5 percent annuity income distribution will produce $17,500 per year or $1,458 per month forever for Keesha. In addition, it allows James to change the beneficiary if Keesha predeceases him, which is not an option with the Bigg Lumber and Supply Co. pension. This policy also has the potential of building some cash value for the couple to access if need be, whereas there is no such benefit available with the company pension plan. Best of all, the $350,000 insurance proceeds could also be invested in something else instead of an annuity that would keep all or some of the principal intact for Keesha to leave as an inheritance to their five children. Of course, James has to be relatively healthy, and Keesha has to feel comfortable with possibly having to continue premiums on this policy while James is still alive if he is unable or unwilling to make payments for some reason.

Their financial advisor helped them explore different methods of dividing pension and retirement plans cleanly and simply. One would be for James to buy out Keesha's pension share with a lump sum cash payment or other marital assets if the marriage dissolved, based on how long they were together. The second option, which James and Keesha agreed made the most sense, was for James to agree in the TA that he would pay Keesha only if and when the pension vested, using a qualified domestic relations order, or QDRO. While neither of them expected to need this clause of their agreement, discussing what was fair and equitable was a good process for them to help build their communication skills and align their values. (Check with your financial advisors before implementing this strategy, as with all ideas presented in this book.)

Appendix 2

Create an "Own and Owe" List

In order for you to plan properly, you need to have a complete listing of all of your financial information—everything that you own and owe. Whether you are working with an attorney or a financial advisor, or planning on your own, a complete listing will help you and your partner plan better and will make it easier for your family later if you are sick or pass away.

First, gather up copies of all the documents listed below in a folder. Second, create a list or spreadsheet summarizing all you own and owe.

What You Own

Accounts or Investments (recent statement)
- Bank accounts (checking, savings, money market, CDs, etc.)
- Investments (brokerage accounts, mutual funds, stocks/bonds)

- Retirement accounts (IRAs, 401(k)s, deferred compensation, etc.)
- Annuities
- Savings bonds or other bonds (paper bonds or statements)
- Individual stocks (paper stock certificates or statements)

Real estate (deed and property tax bill)
- Home
- Rental property
- Business property
- Farm
- Vacation time-share
- Oil, gas, or mineral interests

Vehicle titles
- Car
- Truck
- Boat
- Trailer
- Motorcycle
- RV

Personal property or collectibles (with emotional or dollar value)
- Jewelry
- Antiques
- Tools
- Equipment
- Gold, silver, precious metals
- Sports memorabilia
- Other collectibles

Insurance (recent statements and policies)

- Life insurance
- Homeowners insurance
- Vehicle insurance
- Umbrella insurance
- Long-term care insurance
- Disability insurance

Business documents (articles, bylaws, or operating agreement)
- Corporation
- LLC
- Partnership

Pension plan statements (showing death benefits)

Other assets

Current estate plan documents
- Last will and testament
- Power of attorney for property
- Power of attorney for healthcare or advance directive
- Living will
- Trust

What You Owe

- Home mortgage
- Vehicle loans
- Credit card statements
- Personal or consumer loans
- Unpaid income tax
- Any other bills or debts that are not paid off monthly

Appendix 3

QTIP Trust Case Study

Consider having your attorney draft a trust as part of your Togetherness Agreement.

One very popular type of trust is a qualified terminable interest property trust, or QTIP.

Charles and Katie had two goals when planning their marriage with children. One goal was to provide for each other and the other to make sure that the children from his first marriage receive the inheritance intended. Charles and Katie wanted to make sure that the inheritance received from his recently deceased mother would be held in a trust designed to first help Katie with income at his passing but then to eventually go to the two boys from his previous marriage, and not to pass along to any future spouse of Katie's.

A QTIP is an increasingly popular choice in these cases. Here is why, according to Choudhri: It "allows you to leave your assets to your surviving spouse for the duration of his or her lifetime. When your surviving spouse dies, the assets in the QTIP trust then get passed on to your children or grandchildren"[1] or a charity. In effect, it allows you to control your assets from your grave! You can give your current spouse access to all of the income from the

QTIP while also providing for your children. Moreover, the "QTIP trust allows you to take advantage of the powerful *marital deduction*, which provides that an inheritance one spouse receives from the other is entirely exempt from estate taxes," says Choudhri.[2]

Make sure that you find and work with a qualified trust and estate lawyer like Charles and Katie did to determine whether the QTIP is appropriate in your case. There may be other ways to restructure your estate to achieve all of your estate goals.

Notes

Introduction

1. Throughout this book, names and personal details have been changed to protect identities.

Chapter 1: Taking Stock

1. Ron L. Deal, *The Smart Stepfamily: Seven Steps to a Healthy Family*, revised and expanded edition (Minneapolis: Bethany House Publishers, 2014), provides a comprehensive overview of how to build a strong blended family.

2. For more resources and support, visit www.familylife.com/blended.

3. Brad Hewitt and James Moline, *Your New Money Mindset: Create a Healthy Relationship with Money* (Carol Stream, IL: Tyndale, 2015), 12.

4. Hewitt and Moline, *Your New Money Mindset*, 66. Comment: For most of us, it's easy to believe that a person with $25 million in assets has enough and should feel financially secure. "If I had that much," we tell ourselves, "I'd be content for sure." But what if someone who makes less than you do now suggested that you, too, have enough and should be content? Oh, it's fine when we're talking about what others have, but my subjective assessment of myself is that I have a right to feel insecure. Funny how that works.

5. The items listed in appendix 2 might get your thoughts going.

Chapter 2: Creating a Togetherness Agreement

1. Jessica Mairs, "Conceptual Home for Couples Designed to Split into Two Halves after Divorce," *Dezeen*, July 11, 2016, www.dezeen.com/2016/07/11/pren uptial-housing-omar-kbiri-studio-oba-divorcing-couples-floating-home.

2. Originally, Greg Pettys called the Togetherness Agreement a Shared Covenant Agreement. See Ron L. Deal, *The Smart Stepfamily: Seven Steps to a Healthy Family*, revised and expanded edition (Minneapolis: Bethany House Publishers, 2014), 261–274.

3. Nihara Choudhri, *What to Do Before "I Do": The Modern Couple's Guide to Marriage, Money and Prenups* (Naperville, IL: Sphinx Publishing, 2004), 35.

4. ERISA refers to the Employee Retirement Income Security Act of 1974.

5. As the owner of the policy, Marianne receives the proceeds whether they remain married or divorce, whether Marshall lives or dies. She can benefit from it as her property.

6. An estate attorney or certified financial planner is recommended. There is not a network of Togetherness Agreement advisors. If your advisor is not familiar with the idea of a Togetherness Agreement, share this book with them and direct them to this chapter. Given their training, we trust they will quickly understand the concept and be able to lead you into creating one.

Chapter 3: Merging Yours, Mine, and Ours

1. In the case of physical or emotional abuse, we would want you to seek safety until a clear demonstration of changed behavior is evident. Blind trust is not called for, nor will it help foster emotional safety; trust is possible again after a new track record of behavior is established by the offending person.

2. Personal communication with Ron Deal, January 2018.

Chapter 4: Love and Boundaries

1. W. D. Manning, "Cohabitation and Child Wellbeing," *The Future of Children* 25, no. 2 (Fall 2015): 51–66.

2. Scott Stanley and Galena Rhoades, "Weak and Strong Links: Asymmetrical Commitment in Unmarried Relationships," *Institute for Family Studies*, November 2, 2016, https://ifstudies.org/blog/weak-and-strong-links-asymmetrical-com mitment-in-unmarried-relationships. For further study, see the research by Scott Stanley available at http://slidingvsdeciding.blogspot.com.

3. See Ron's book *Dating and the Single Parent* (Minneapolis: Bethany House, 2012) for a full discussion of cohabitation, dating with kids, and ways to clearly define boundaries in dating.

4. For more information on effective conflict resolution in marriage, see Ron L. Deal and David H. Olson, *The Smart Stepfamily Marriage: Keys to Success in the Blended Family* (Minneapolis: Bethany House, 2015).

5. Edwin H. Friedman, *A Failure of Nerve: Leadership in the Age of the Quick Fix*, ed. Margaret M. Treadwell and Edward W. Beal (New York: Church Publishing, Inc., 2007), 211.

Chapter 5: Money and Former Spouses

1. Robert E. Emery, *Two Homes, One Childhood: A Parenting Plan to Last a Lifetime* (New York: Avery, 2016), 25.

2. Adapted from E. Mark Cummings and Patrick T. Davies, *Marital Conflict and Children: An Emotional Security Perspective* (New York: The Guilford Press, 2010), as referenced in Robert E. Emery, *Two Homes, One Childhood*, 40–42.

3. Kimberly King, in Geoff Williams, "How to Split Parenting Expenses with Your Ex," *U.S. News & World Report*, July 23, 2015, https://money.usnews.co m/money/personal-finance/articles/2015/07/23/how-to-split-parenting-expenses -with-your-ex.

4. Williams, "How to Split Parenting Expenses."

5. Emery, *Two Homes, One Childhood*, 179–180.

6. Emery, *Two Homes, One Childhood*, 65–66.

7. For more tips on effective co-parenting, see Ron L. Deal, *The Smart Stepfamily: Seven Steps to a Healthy Family*, revised and expanded edition (Minneapolis: Bethany House, 2014).

8. Adapted from "How to Discuss Money with an Ex," *Money*, November 19, 2013, http://time.com/money/2794912/how-to-discuss-money-with-an-ex.

Chapter 7: Parenting Adult Children and Caring for Aging Parents

1. Alan Dunn, "Failure to Launch: Adult Children Moving Back Home," *Forbes*, June 6, 2012, www.forbes.com/sites/moneywisewomen/2012/06/06/failure -to-launch-adult-children-moving-back-home/#2b50cea017ba.

2. For more on wise dating practices and making decisions about forming a blended family, read Ron's book *Dating and the Single Parent* (Minneapolis: Bethany House, 2012).

3. Emily E. Wiemers, Judith A. Seltzer, Robert F. Schoeni, V. Joseph Hotz, and Suzanne M. Bianchi, *Stepfamily Structure and Transfers between Generations in U.S. Families* (paper presentation, 2015 annual meeting of the Population Association of America, San Diego, CA, updated July 2018), 24–25, http://public.econ .duke.edu/~vjh3/working_papers/StepkinTransfers.pdf.

Chapter 8: Planning Your Child's Education

1. "Highlights" in "Trends in Higher Education," College Board, April 4, 2019, https://trends.collegeboard.org/college-pricing/highlights.

2. Ipsos Public Affairs for Sallie Mae, *How America Pays for Graduate School 2017*, 2, www.salliemae.com/assets/Research/HAPGS/HAPGRAD_School Report.pdf.

3. Anthony P. Carnevale, Nicole Smith, and Jeff Strohl, *Recovery: Job Growth and Education Requirements Through 2020*, Executive Summary (Washington, DC: Georgetown Public Policy Institute), 3, www.columbiagreenworks.org/Re covery2020.pdf.

4. Christopher R. Tamborini, ChangHwan Kim, and Arthur Sakamoto, "Education and Lifetime Earnings in the United States," *Demography* 52, no. 4 (August 2015), 1383–1407. See www.ssa.gov/policy/docs/research-summaries/education -earnings.html.

5. Ipsos Public Affairs for Sallie Mae, *How America Pays for College 2017*, 8, www.salliemae.com/assets/Research/HAP/HowAmericaPaysforCollege2017.pdf.

6. Complete College America, *Four-Year Myth: Make College Affordable. Restore the Promise of Graduating on Time* (Indianapolis, IN: 2014), 6, https:// completecollege.org/wp-content/uploads/2017/05/4-Year-Myth.pdf.

7. One of the unique benefits of a 529 is a special gift tax exclusion. A person can contribute a onetime "superfunding" gift to a 529 of up to five times the annual gift tax exclusion (currently $75,000, based on the $15,000 annual exclusion in 2019). While numbers like that may be out of reach for most families today, it's sometimes a helpful option for downsizing grandparents who want to support their grandchildren and possibly reduce later estate taxes.

8. Distributions from an IRA before age 59½ are not subject to a 10 percent penalty if used for qualified higher education expenses. See Sarah Brenner, "Tapping an IRA to Pay Education Expenses? Avoid These 4 Mistakes," *Ed Slott and Company, LLC*, December 14, 2015, www.irahelp.com/slottreport/tapping-ira-pay -education-expenses.

9. The College Board, *Trends in College Pricing 2016*, October 2016, 9, https:// trends.collegeboard.org/sites/default/files/2016-trends-college-pricing-web_0.pdf.

10. Michelle Singletary, "Your Child Probably Won't Get a Full Ride to College," October 16, 2018, *The Washington Post*, www.washingtonpost.com /business/2018/10/16/odds-your-child-getting-full-ride-college-are-low.

11. Conducted by Ipsos Public Affairs for Sallie Mae, *How America Pays for College 2018*, 2, www.salliemae.com/assets/research/HAP/HowAmericaPaysfor College2018.pdf.

12. Abigail Hess, "Here's How Much the Average Student Loan Borrower Owes When They Graduate," *CNBC*, February 15, 2018, www.cnbc.com/2018 /02/15/heres-how-much-the-average-student-loan-borrower-owes-when-they -graduate.html.

13. "Responsible Student Loan Borrowing," Edvisors, April 3, 2019, www.ed visors.com/college-loans/choosing-loans/responsible-borrowing.

14. "ACT/SAT Differences," Better Prep Success, April 5, 2019, https://better prepsuccess.com/info/act-sat-differences.

15. "ACT Prep Live Classes Available in Central Illinois," Better Prep Success, April 5, 2019, https://betterprepsuccess.com/courses/act-prep-class.

Chapter 9: Planning Your Retirement

1. "Life Expectancy Home Page," Social Security, April 4, 2019, www.ssa.gov /planners/lifeexpectancy.html.

2. Employee Benefit Research Institute and Greenwald & Associates, *2018 Retirement Confidence Survey*, April 24, 2018, 11, www.ebri.org/docs/default -source/rcs/1_2018rcs_report_v5mgachecked.pdf?sfvrsn=e2e9302f_2.

3. Lisa Greenwald, Greenwald & Associates, Craig Copeland, and Jack Van-Derhei, Newsletter #431, Employee Benefit Research Institute.

4. "Risk" in this context is defined as volatility and the resulting degree of potential loss of our investment principal. A risk profile is how we perceive and feel about investment risks, because we all have different philosophies about our relationship with the potential loss of capital.

5. "Frequently Asked Questions About 401(k) Plan Research," Investment Company Institute, March 2019, www.ici.org/policy/retirement/plan/401k/faqs _401k.

. 6. The following information is adapted from Jim Blankenship, *A Social Security Owner's Manual*, 4th ed. (CreateSpace, 2019). Used with permission.

7. Benefits are based on the amount of earned wages over one's working years.

Chapter 10: Planning for Healthcare Needs

1. "How Much Care Will You Need?" LongTermCare.gov, US Department of Health and Human Services, accessed February 20, 2019, https://longtermcare.acl.gov/the-basics/how-much-care-will-you-need.html.

2. The term "healthcare power of attorney" or "healthcare POA" can be used to refer to the document used to name your agent or the person you named as your agent. For instance, "You need to sign a healthcare power of attorney." Or the nurse at the hospital might say, "We need to call their healthcare power of attorney."

3. "How Much Care Will You Need?" LongTermCare.gov, US Department of Health and Human Services, accessed February 20, 2019, https://longtermcare.acl.gov/the-basics/how-much-care-will-you-need.html.

4. Social Security disability benefits can also provide income, but those benefits come only after a slow application process, and the benefits ultimately received are usually only a fraction of the income being earned prior to the disability. Private disability insurance can help close the gap between Social Security disability and household expenses, and can usually be received much more quickly than Social Security.

Chapter 11: Planning Your Estate

1. Jeffrey M. Jones, "Majority in U.S. Do Not Have a Will," Gallup, May 18, 2016, www.gallup.com/poll/191651/majority-not.aspx.

Appendix 3: QTIP Trust Case Study

1. Nihara Choudhri, *What to Do Before "I Do": The Modern Couple's Guide to Marriage, Money and Prenups* (Naperville, IL: Sphinx Publishing, 2004), 66.

2. Choudhri, *What to Do*, 66.

Ron L. Deal is a marriage and family author, speaker, and therapist. He is founder of Smart Stepfamilies™, the director of FamilyLife Blended® (a division of FamilyLife®), and the author/coauthor of numerous books, including *The Smart Stepfamily Marriage*, *The Smart Stepmom*, *The Smart Stepdad*, *Dating and the Single Parent*, and the bestselling *The Smart Stepfamily*. In addition, he is the consulting editor of the SMART STEPFAMILY SERIES and has published over a dozen videos and study resources and hundreds of magazine and online articles. His work has been quoted or referenced by many news outlets such as the *New York Times*, the *Wall Street Journal*, and *USA Today*. Ron's books, podcast, conference events, social media presence, online resources, and one-minute radio feature, *FamilyLife Blended* (heard daily on hundreds of stations nationwide and online), make him the leading voice on blended families in the US. He is a licensed marriage and family therapist who frequently appears in the national media, including *FamilyLife Today* and *Focus on the Family*, and he conducts marriage and family seminars around the country and internationally. He and his wife, Nan, have three boys. For more information, go to SmartStepfamilies.com.

Greg S. Pettys, CLU, ChFC, CFP, has thirty-four years of specialized experience in securities and life insurance sales and services. He has provided life insurance point-of-sale and wholesaling services with estate planning and wealth transfer expertise to over one thousand financial advisors across the country with national financial service companies, including Edward Jones, State Farm,

Morgan Stanley, Wells Fargo, Raymond James, Woodbury Financial, and Mass Mutual. Greg has lived on three continents and travels on mission extensively to India. He and his wife, Johnita, have six children. Ron has known Greg for twenty years, and Greg speaks regularly at Ron's Smart Stepfamily events.

David O. Edwards is an estate planning and elder law attorney based in Springfield, Illinois. He has practiced law for more than twenty years and has extensive experience working with families who have concerns about passing their estate to their loved ones as well as providing long-term care for their parents and themselves. He and his wife, Michelle, have two children. David speaks regularly at Ron's Smart Stepfamily events. David coaches blended families on legal and financial matters. For more information go to blendedfamilyfinances.com.

More Resources for the Smart Stepfamily

Visit smartstepfamilies.com and familylifeblended.com for additional information.

Providing practical, realistic solutions to the unique issues that stepfamilies face, Ron Deal helps remarried couples solve the everyday challenges of stepparenting and shares seven steps to raising a healthy family.

The Smart Stepfamily by Ron L. Deal

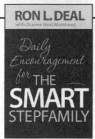

These 365 short and sweet thoughts, specifically for stepfamilies, will keep your family blending and bonding throughout the year. Each daily dose of encouragement includes a prayer for your home. Sharing these readings with your spouse and, when appropriate, kids will spark valuable conversations that foster family understanding and closeness.

Daily Encouragement for the Smart Stepfamily by Ron L. Deal with Dianne Neal Matthews

Using information from a national remarriage survey, leading experts Ron Deal and David Olson show couples how to strengthen their new marriage and overcome common challenges. Whether you're dating, engaged, a young stepfamily, or an empty-nest couple, *The Smart Stepfamily Marriage* gives you the tools you need at any stage to create a remarriage that will last.

The Smart Stepfamily Marriage by Ron L. Deal and David H. Olson

⟨⟩BETHANYHOUSE

You May Also Like. . .

Stepfamily experts Ron L. Deal and Laura Petherbridge show you how to survive and thrive as a stepmom, including how to be a positive influence on the children and how to deal with conflict, as well as practical issues like dealing with holidays and between-home communication.

The Smart Stepmom by Ron L. Deal and Laura Petherbridge

Here is the survival guide every stepfather needs to succeed. Ron Deal equips stepdads everywhere with advice on everything—from how to connect with your stepchildren to handling tricky issues such as discipline and dealing with your wife's ex.

The Smart Stepdad by Ron L. Deal

In the eight-session DVD—ideal for small groups, seminars, or individual couples—expert Ron Deal offers usable solutions for everyday living, practical tips for raising stepkids, and ways to strengthen your marriage.

The Smart Stepfamily DVD by Ron L. Deal

BETHANYHOUSE